POCKET
MARKETING

The
Economist
Books

POCKET
MARKETING

THE ECONOMIST IN ASSOCIATION WITH
PROFILE BOOKS LTD

Profile Books Ltd, Registered Office:
62 Queen Anne Street, London W1M 9LA

First published by Profile Books Ltd
in association with
The Economist Newspaper Ltd 1997

Contributors Tim Hindle, Michael Thomas

Printed by
LEGO S.p.a. - Vicenza - Italy

A CIP catalogue record for this book is available
from the British Library

ISBN 1 86197 020 X

CONTENTS

INTRODUCTION

Pocket Marketing is one in a series of management guides that brings the clarity and wit for which *The Economist* is famous to the concepts, practicalities and skills involved in running a business.

It is divided into three parts.

Part 1 includes essays on consumers, advertising, brands and electronic commerce.

Part 2 is an A–Z of the main terms that those directly involved in marketing products and services use or encounter in their everyday working life, but which they may not always feel that they fully understand.

Throughout this section are a number of checklists to help managers, aspiring managers and marketing professionals in their daily business. The book is sprinkled with revealing nuggets of information about companies and products. These show that business is a broad human endeavour with plenty of room for wit and creativity as well as for triumph and disappointment.

In this section words in small capitals usually indicate a separate entry, thus enabling readers to find other relevant information. Note, though, that abbreviations such as IBM are also in small capitals.

Part 3 consists of appendixes with statistical information on, for example, advertising agencies and brands together with an extensive reading list.

The Pocket Management series is designed to take the mystique out of business jargon in a stimulating and entertaining way. Other titles in the series are:

Pocket Accounting
Pocket Director
Pocket Employer
Pocket Information Technology
Pocket Investor
Pocket Law

Pocket Manager
Pocket Marketing
Pocket MBA
Pocket Negotiator
Pocket Strategy
Pocket Telecommunications

Part 1
ESSAYS

CONSUMERS GET REAL

Marketing textbooks have been rewritten in recent years by a dramatic shift in the supply and demand for goods and services. When America's consumer champion Ralph Nader criticised the Chevrolet Corsair's unsafe welding, he almost single-handedly forced the manufacturer to withdraw the car from the market. And that marked a significant turning point, the change from a time when manufacturers could sell almost any old rubbish that they could produce, to a time when consumers could force to the wall almost any firm that did not produce goods or services of the very highest quality.

That process has not ended. Consumers today are more demanding than ever. And marketing is, more than ever, all about understanding what those demands are, and how they can most efficiently be satisfied.

It was no coincidence that the first generation to be put under the microscope by the marketing professionals was the generation beginning to gather spending power as Nader was liberating consumers from the manufacturers' stranglehold. The much-discussed baby boomers, the generation born in the immediate aftermath of the second world war, have had their wants and needs put under the microscope like no other generation before them.

And like no generation after them, until, that is, the very latest age group to hit the tills with money in their pockets. Generation X, christened after a best-selling book of the same name by Douglas Coupland, is the generation born between 1967 and 1981, the children of the baby boomers. As one American commentator put it: "They are the first generation in American history to realise that they will not enjoy a higher standard of living than their parents". Whether that turns out to be true or not, it is the perception that counts.

Generation Xers are found all over the western world, and beyond. In Britain, they're better known as "get-a-lifers", seekers after a more holistic existence than the single-minded, money-maximising, divorce-prone role model that they were offered by their parents.

In Coupland's novel, the original Generation Xers were a cynical bunch, drifting from one low-value McJob to another. Even in his later novel, Microserfs, depicting the Generation Xers at "real" work – real work in the 1990s being beneath Bill's beady gaze (Bill Gates, that is) – there is an unremitting tedium to the round of late-night deadline-induced programming, junk meals and aimless car journeys.

But although this generation spurns the conspicuous consumption of their predecessors, marketers have not failed to realise that Generation Xers are not averse to consumption *per se* They have their own consumer magazines and certain manufacturers have very successfully struck a chord with them. They are not the Guccis or Louis Vuittons who set the fashion trend a decade ago. Rather they are firms like Nike, Calvin Klein and Diesel jeans, firms that blur gender distinctions, sell a "real" world of drugs and anorexia, and don't take their market for a fool.

As Nike said in one of its advertisements: "We don't sell dreams. We sell shoes," – the very antithesis of the famous pitch of the Revlon chairman who once asked his sales force what business they thought they were in. They all replied, "The business of selling cosmetics". "No," replied the Revlon man, without the hint of a smile. "You're in the business of selling dreams." Well, he might be surprised to find that does not go far with today's Generation Xers.

Indeed, so "real" is the advertising of some of these firms that the most famous baby boomer of them all, President Bill Clinton, has berated it for enticing American youth too far towards the glazed-over look adopted by the "real" models that appear in it.

Nostalgia boom
Baby boomers are the wealthiest generation ever

to have lived. In the UK, the 45-55 age group accounts for 13% of the population but for 23% of its expenditure. In spite of this, however, much market research suggests that they are not a happy bunch. By now they are supposed to be "empty nesters" whose children have left to build homes of their own. Still healthy and active, they are also due to inherit what are (historically) small fortunes from their longer-living parents. They should right now be in the middle of a spending bonanza the likes of which the world has never seen.

For many of them though, it has not worked out like that. The recession of the early 1990s left them feeling poorer, even if statistically that was an illusion. To feel more comfortable, they adjusted their personal balance sheets, shedding debt and improving the mix of their assets. After the blow-out of the 1980s, consumers began to save more and to spend less.

On top of which, and much to their surprise, the baby boomers find themselves still tied down by the responsibility of elderly parents whose life expectancy has exceeded every actuary's expectations, and by Generation X children whose lifestyle too often seems to include every experience except that of the workplace. Moreover, as they watch the safety net of the welfare state being rapidly unwound around them, the baby boomers are becoming deeply anxious about their own financial security in their old age.

Surprisingly, the baby boomers and their children have several things in common. They like the same music: the parents waxing lyrical about the Beatles, while their offspring listen to Oasis and other Lennon and McCartney sound-alikes. Even in the cinema, the moody young heroes of today bear a not accidental resemblance to James Dean and the young Marlon Brando.

Finally, both generations are equally disinterested in computers and their trappings. Generation Xers' disinterest arises from knowledge. They have been into computers and found what they represent to be lacking. Computers cut them off from the "real" world and from all the other things that they need to fit into their lives – things like "friends", and it is no coincidence that a television show with that title proved to be one of the most popular programmes with Generation Xers.

Baby boomers have shied away from computers too, but for different reasons. They are afraid that they might not be able to grasp their full potential, and starting to learn to use a keyboard at their age is like starting to learn a foreign language – full of embarrassing incidents and humbling mistakes that they do not wish to handle.

THE RENAISSANCE OF THE BRAND

There was a peculiar cult about in the 1980s which, for want of a better name, could be called "brand worship". Its core belief was that brand names had a great and immutable value that most people had failed to appreciate. It found some of its keenest followers in Europe, which was stuffed with fine old-name products suffering a similar fate as its fine old-name aristocrats.

Hidden assets

When in 1988 the Swiss food-products company Nestlé bought the British confectionery group Rowntree, the price paid included well over $1bn for something that had never appeared on Rowntree's balance sheet: the value of some of the names in its portfolio of products, like Polo, Kit-Kat and After Eight.

As this hidden value became more widely recognised, a number of companies decided to put the value of their brands on to their balance sheet. The drinks and hotels group Grand Metropolitan added £500m for a few of its more recently acquired products, such as Smirnoff vodka. When Polly Peck bought the Del Monte fresh-fruits business it added £250m to its assets for the value of the Del Monte name alone. (Polly Peck subsequently collapsed, in part because it overstretched itself with the Del Monte purchase.) This practice was not just cosmetic. It improved the companies' gearing and, as a consequence, their ability to borrow from banks, and thence their capacity to buy yet more brands.

Reputation is all

However, events conspired to bring the brand-worshippers down to earth. The value of brands was seen to be far less tangible than the accountants who were using it to puff up balance sheets might have wished. For a start, names can go off faster than a raw steak in Riyadh: sales of Perrier water were decimated in 1990 by the discovery of small quantities of benzene in samples taken from the water's source.

Likewise the great name of Salomon Brothers was humbled overnight by the discovery in 1991 of dirty dealing in its US government securities department. Salomon had few assets but its name and a bunch of screens. Full-page newspaper advertisements with a Japanese-style confession from its new chairman, Warren Buffett, went some way towards restoring the value of the Salomon brand of securities business.

Own-brand growth

It was not just the vulnerability of brands to unexpected events that reduced their glamour. Two market-related events were also working against them. In consumer goods, retailers were gaining the upper hand in their eternal power struggle with manufacturers.

The powerful retail chains found that one way of increasing their profit margins was to have "own-label" products specially manufactured for them. Consumers came to value the Safeways name on a bottle of wine, or Marks & Spencer's St Michael label on a bar of chocolate, quite as highly as the names of any of the well-established manufacturers of these products.

In a time of recession, consumers were even more attracted to own-label products by their price. This was always lower than the famous-name manufacturers. For the balance-sheet value of these manufacturers' brands always lay essentially in the premium that they could charge for sticking their name on the product. That premium could be as high as 50%, and it was always bound to attract pot-shots.

By the mid 1990s, the pot-shots were coming from all directions. Big supermarkets turned their gaze not just towards food and drink but to banking and insurance and other financial services. The Virgin group became a by-word for "brand stretching", for taking a name and planting it on any product or service where there were fat margins or a complacent oligopoly. There was Virgin cola, Virgin insurance, a Virgin radio station and a Virgin airline. There seemed to be few industries off-limits to the name.

Global dreams
Another setback for traditional brands came from the unexpected difficulties they found in taking brands across borders. In the excitement of globalisation, companies anticipated making huge economies of scale from marketing the same brand in the same way right across the globe. Any product with a strong market share in one country was fair game for globalisation. If products that are as American as McDonald's and Coca-Cola could do it, then anybody could.

They could not, of course, because not all names travel well. For example, Irish Mist liqueur has a hard time in German-speaking markets (mist in German means manure). Moreover, within the global village that marketing people were blindly assuming already existed, distinct tastes were proving remarkably persistent. While Coca-Cola was a big success in South Africa, PepsiCo bowed out of the country after three difficult years.

Unilever, which had traditionally allowed its national detergent companies great autonomy to develop their own products, came under the influence of the globalisers and reversed its policy for the launch of Radion, a detergent that was sold on its ability to remove odours as well as dirt. With Radion the company imposed a universally uniform package design and a bright orange colour on, in many cases, reluctant national managers.

Since then Unilever has reached a compromise with its international brands. It defines what it sees as a product's "core brand values", those which meet common needs in all its main markets, and it then tinkers with other aspects of the brand according to the needs of different local markets.

The need to nurture
The main lesson of the cult of the brand, and of its downfall, is that brands cannot be left unattended

for long. Building them up is a long, hard process and so is maintaining them; a fact that has been ignored by those who have bought an already established brand in the belief that with such-and-such a name they cannot go wrong.

Look at the products on the supermarket shelves that have not had their market shares drastically eroded by own-label products. They include instant coffee and breakfast cereals. The likes of Nescafé and Kellogg have retained their market leadership because they have spent much of the premium in their prices on constantly developing new products and on improving existing ones. Then they have spent even more on advertising the fact. The brand that is merely sat upon will soon be squashed.

But there are no guarantees even for those brands that are not sat upon. A recent report from the Boston Consulting Group says, "Many brands today are dying. Not the natural death of absence but the slow, painful death of sales and margin erosion. The managers of these brands are not complacent – in fact they are constantly tweaking the advertising, pricing and cost of their brands. At the heart of the problem is a more fundamental issue: can the original promise of the brand be recreated and a new spark lit with today's consumers? We believe it can. Most brands can be reinvented through brand renaissance."

ADVERTISING

The advertising industry, as much as its own inventions, lives off the impression that it creates. Part of that impression used to be that advertising was a worthy profession based on much research into consumer behaviour, and even more understanding of it. Anybody who knows that women in New York use nearly 30 times as much make-up as women in Vermont must surely know more about consumers than consumers know about themselves.

But the impression that the advertising industry has given in recent years has been rather different: it has been the impression of an industry obsessed with growth at almost any price; and willing to follow any fad for a quick profit.

Keeping up is hard to do

Admittedly the industry has had to cope with unprecedented pressures to perform. That has made it an enthusiastic follower of the fashion to "go global". When multinational clients, like Unilever and Gillette, demanded that the same advertising agency serve them in all their markets, the agencies by and large obliged. Wherever Unilever has gone (which is just about everywhere) so has its main agency, J. Walter Thompson. In Europe alone JWT has offices in more than 15 countries.

At the same time the agencies have been trying to come to grips with the death of the "mass market", a sort of essential yeast extract on which they all grew up. Early advertisements were designed to sell Singer sewing machines, Model T Fords, or whatever, in one way to everybody. The economies of scale that enabled companies like Singer and Ford to produce for a mass market also worked in favour of their agencies. The high cost of creating their advertisements could be spread by using the same advertisements widely.

The principle carried into globalisation; indeed one of its main attractions for manufacturers and their agencies was the further economies of scale that it promised. If one advertisement could sell the same product to a housewife in Maine and to a black child in Louisiana, then it could also sell the product to mothers in Paris, children in Prague and housewives in Hong Kong. Or so the argument went.

Unfortunately for the agencies, just as they were going global their idea of the mass market was having to be revised. For industry had discovered "segmentation": the phenomenon of a post mass-market era in which sophisticated production methods enabled the same product to be "tweaked" almost without limit. That way it could be made to appeal to a large number of small market segments. A fairly uniform commodity-type product like Tylenol, a US over-the-counter drug for headaches, was suddenly extended to include 40 different varieties of the drug, each targeted at a slightly different consumer.

Even the Ford Escort car, rolling off production lines that had invented the mass market, became available in a wide range of models: souped-up models for aggressive make-believe rally driver; stylish cabriolets for those whose hair looked good in a high wind; and solid reliable models for drivers whose main outing was a weekly trip to collect their pension.

Segmentation was followed by "customisation". Levis, for example, began to take customers' measurements, put them into a computer and cut their cloth accordingly. The bespoke 501 was born. Likewise, it was said of one BMW model that no two cars were exactly the same, so numerous were the opportunities for customisation.

Customisation and segmentation were accompanied by another change that had a strong influence on the advertising industry: the shortening of products' life-cycles. For a while nothing was meant to last; all goods were fashion goods, designed to be thrown away as the seasons changed. Swatch turned the watch into a fashion item; and a *Wall Street Journal* headline declared, "IBM to start announcing its fall line".

Open skies

At the same time the channels through which advertisers told the world about their products were changing. A new enthusiasm for deregulating the airwaves brought a host of new television and radio stations, especially in Europe where the state's monopoly of broadcasting had been traditionally tight.

The new stations fought fiercely for advertising's dollars, and they were fighting not only with each other but also with commercial radio. Setting up a radio station requires very little capital, and in some countries it sometimes seems as if there are as many channels as there are listeners.

Advertisers trying to reach segmented markets favoured media with narrow identifiable audiences – black teenagers, women aged 35–45, and so on – and the media obliged. "Narrowcasting" grew at the expense of broadcasting. Television provided sports channels, pop-music channels and pre-war movie channels. Radio could cast even more narrowly, reaching (should any advertiser want to) a few hundred jazz fans, or even the 33 people who had not liked any music since Elvis died.

In this "narrow" world, Levi's could appear in *Vogue* as a high-fashion item for the richest people on earth at the same time as it was seen on city-centre billboards as a garment for the urban underclass.

Media barony

While television and radio were being deregulated into more and more providers of services, the printed media were becoming more concentrated into ever bigger groups. The likes of Murdoch, Time Warner and Bertelsmann created vast media empires that were no respecters of any division between print and film.

These empires threatened the delicate balance of power between advertisers and the media. For as they used their muscle to push up their advertising rates, the agencies responded by pooling their "media buying" divisions to gain economies of scale and to have more clout in bargaining with the media barons.

On top of all this came the Internet. And the traditional agencies were slow to appreciate its potential, leaving its "pages" and communications to be created by computer buffs.

The Net was not the only ground to be vacated by the agencies. They suddenly found themselves competing with management consultancies for the high ground of their business. Major clients would as happily turn to McKinsey to discuss their brand development as they would to their advertising agency.

It has been a rough few years for the old-established advertising firms. They have had to watch their back, their front, and their sides, and there are few signs that they can let their vigilance slip in the years to come.

THE PITFALLS OF ELECTRONIC COMMERCE

In the few years since the Internet has taken off, the slow growth of electronic commerce has been one of its greatest disappointments. Consumers are faced with a bewildering choice of thousands of online stores, each one inadequate in its own way. Just finding something to buy is a triumph, never mind comparing prices and paying for it. Between the endless lists of online merchants and the delays as each graphics-heavy shopfront downloads, you can spend an hour just finding a product. No wonder analysts reckon that consumer Internet transactions in 1996 were worth a total of only around $500 million – $600 million, about the same as was spent on computer publications full of glowing articles on Internet commerce.

But it will get better – much better – and in ways that today's fitful efforts only hint at. Indeed, practically everything that was predicted about electronic commerce three years ago has turned out to be wrong.

For starters the big money is not in consumer shopping but in business-to-business commerce. This should not have been a surprise – it mirrors the physical world, where business transactions are worth about ten times as much as consumer sales – but few realised how quickly apparently stodgy firms would convert. The reason: most business transactions were already done at a distance, whether by fax, telephone, post, or private electronic links. Moving that process to the Internet makes it cheaper, faster and easier.

Second, the industry has defined electronic commerce too narrowly. Most analysts include only transactions actually carried out on the Internet; but many consumers research their purchases online and then buy in some other way. Only 3% of business-to-business Web sites are designed for direct sales, rather than for marketing and customer service, says Forrester research, a Massachusetts consultancy. Even for consumer businesses, only 9% of sites offer online transactions.

Third, the online leaders are not the traditional commercial giants of the physical world, but outsiders who often knew next to nothing about the markets they chose to enter. They succeeded because they understood the Internet and how it could be harnessed to commerce of any sort.

The most important lesson would-be traders on the Internet must learn is that it rarely works like the physical world. For example, the "virtual malls" that have sprung up in their thousands over the past two years have been an abject failure. In real life, where driving to the store can take as long as shopping itself, putting many unrelated stores under one roof is a good way to attract a critical mass of customers. Online, where no store is more than a mouse click from any other, the hope was that the reputation of the mall itself would draw the punters in from the chaos online. But big firms chose to stand alone, and smaller stores are increasingly grouping themselves by theme, joining or creating consumer communities with shared interests. Some have taken to advertising in stores selling related goods, which is rarely done in the real world.

Advertising and marketing

Despite the slow take-off of electronic commerce, advertising and marketing are being profoundly changed by it. This is because the Internet, unlike any advertising vehicle before it, is an interactive medium, completely customised for each viewer.

The implications of this are just starting to sink in. Where they will be felt most is in the target market known as the "hard middle". Jeff Bezos of pioneering electronic bookseller Amazon, defines it like this: "In today's world, if you want to reach 12 people, that's easy: you use the phone. If you want to reach 12 million people, it's easy: you take out an ad during the Superbowl. But if you want to pitch something to 10,000 people – the hard middle – that's really hard."

Today's answer to the hard middle is direct

mail, which is expensive and inefficient. The Internet makes it easier both to target potentially interested consumers and to communicate with them. Search services such as InfoSeek, for example, sell keywords: search for "airline tickets", and an ad banner for American Express's travel service shows up on top of the resulting list. Call it advertising or direct marketing – the distinctions are blurring. Indeed, First Virtual, an Internet commerce firm, has developed an advertisement that can act as a tiny shopfront (imagine a Nike ad that would let you order a pair of shoes from within the banner), merging advertising and direct commerce.

An Internet ad banner provides a direct link to the advertiser's site, offering interested consumers an easy way to go there for more information or an opportunity to buy. Compare that with a television ad, which has to create such an impression that you remember it days later when you are shopping. Because online advertising offers the capacity for an immediate response, it challenges the old saw that merchants know that only half of their advertising works, but not which half. On the Internet it is easy to know which half: just count the "click-throughs".

Indeed, last year Procter & Gamble refused to pay for ads that people did not click on. Web sites were outraged (what if it was just a lame ad?), but one way or another advertisers will demand more evidence of effectiveness in future.

Total Internet advertising revenues in 1996 were just $267 million, compared with $33 billion spent on television advertising in America alone – even though top Internet sites have television-sized audiences of a million viewers a day. America Online, with 8 million subscribers the biggest Internet service provider, has more viewers than any cable television network or newspaper, and all but the world's two most popular magazines. So where is the big advertising money that Internet media companies are expecting? Waiting and seeing: the market is too new for advertisers yet to be sure that they will get their money's worth.

Part 2
A–Z

A CLASSIFICATION OF RESIDENTIAL NEIGHBOURHOODS

A system of categorising residential areas, known commonly by its acronym ACORN, developed in the late 1970s.

Within ACORN there are 39 different neighbourhood types. They range from "agricultural villages" to "unimproved terraces with old people"; and from "recent private housing (young families)" to "older private housing (skilled workers)".

ACORN is widely believed to provide a better basis for predicting consumer behaviour than alternative methods of classifying HOUSEHOLDS – such as, for example, according to the occupation of the main breadwinner. ACORN has been used widely by banks and retailers to determine where to locate new outlets; and it has been much used by market researchers looking for samples for their questionnaires.

ABC

See AUDIT BUREAU OF CIRCULATION.

A/B/C1

A classification used for different social groups (see SOCIAL GRADING). Although it originated in the UK, it has been exported to other countries through the international influence of UK advertising agencies.

ABOVE-THE-LINE

That part of a company's MARKETING BUDGET that is spent on ADVERTISING in the MEDIA as opposed to other activities like sales PROMOTION and DIRECT MARKETING. These are (emotively and much to the disgust of their practitioners) described as BELOW-THE-LINE.

The origin of the "line" probably lies in accounting terminology. Marketers talk of "crossing the line" when referring to their attempts to create INTEGRATED COMMUNICATIONS.

ACCOUNT DIRECTOR

The top manager in an ADVERTISING AGENCY; the

person in charge of the team within the agency that is responsible for an account (a client). Each client has a team and each team has an account director.

The account director co-ordinates the various functions represented in a typical team; for example, CREATIVE, MEDIA and MARKET RESEARCH. Depending on the size of the agency, and also on the size of the client, the account director may work with an account manager. The account manager is responsible for day-to-day liaison between the client and the various departments within the agency.

ACHIEVER

A category of American consumer from the widely used VALS classification (see also LIFESTYLE).

ACORN

See A CLASSIFICATION OF RESIDENTIAL NEIGHBOURHOODS.

Adidas shoes are named after their founder, a German called Adolf Dassler. Adolf was known to his friends as Adi Das-sler. Despite being an abbreviation of a proper name, the trademark is always spelt with a lower case "a": adidas.

ACTION PLAN

A blow-by-blow description of the tactics devised to achieve a particular marketing strategy. An action plan includes schedules of what has to be done when, how and by whom.

An action plan should typically include:

❑ times and places of specific promotions of the PRODUCT (for example, special SAMPLE offers, POINT-OF-SALE displays, or coupons);
❑ trade shows to be attended;
❑ ADVERTISING campaigns to be launched; and
❑ PUBLICITY releases to be distributed.

It should also include a budget for each type of PROMOTION.

ADOPTION

The process by which consumers adopt a new PRODUCT, fashion or idea. Adoption can only happen after consumers have passed through the following stages:

- **Awareness.** Consumers are first made aware of the new product's existence.
- **Interest.** Consumers' interest in the product is titillated by ADVERTISING and PROMOTION.
- **Evaluation.** Consumers evaluate the product in relation to their own needs and desires.
- **Trial.** Consumers have been hooked enough to go out and try the product.
- **Adoption.** Consumers continue to buy the product regularly.

ADSPEND

The total amount spent on ADVERTISING, be it by a company or a country, or in a single ADVERTISING CAMPAIGN.

ADSTOCK

The sum total of the effect of an advertisement, based on an assumption that advertisements leave a trace for some time after they have actually been perceived. This continuing effect is measured quantitatively by applying a gradual decay rate to measures of the advertisement's impact while it is showing (see DAGMAR).

ADVERTISING

A key part of MARKETING, but far from being (as is often assumed) the sum total of it. Advertising is the use of MEDIA to inform consumers about something and/or to persuade them to do something. In effect, it brings products and consumers together, and then modulates the relationship between them.

Communication is a central part of the advertising business, but the industry has not been fully successful at communicating its own value. It is widely criticised for creating illusory desires in consumers to the sole benefit of industrial corporations.

There is a contradiction in the general public's attitude to advertising. On the one hand it is seen as manipulative and cunning (as in SUBLIMINAL ADVERTISING); on the other hand it is seen as unfocused and crude. It can, of course, be both; but not at the same time.

Most professional advertising is not haphazard. Different approaches and different messages are required for different stages of the relationship between consumer and PRODUCT. One classification of these stages is called the HIERARCHY OF EFFECTS. Another is known by the mnemonic AIDA (attention, interest, desire, action).

Advertising is not solely concerned with commercial products. In most countries producers of goods and services account for about half of all advertising expenditure. The other half is spent by marketing intermediaries (such as retailers and banks), by governments in all their guises, by organisations such as charities, and by individuals (in a CLASSIFIED ADVERTISEMENT, for example).

ADVERTISING AGENCY

A firm that handles the ADVERTISING needs of a number of clients. The agency is an intermediary between the producer of goods or services and the MEDIA that will communicate the producer's message to the consumer.

A typical modern agency will have a number of different departments.

Advertising is the most fun you can have with your clothes on.

Jerry Della Femina, advertising agency founder

• **Research.** To provide MARKET RESEARCH relevant to the agency's clients. Data on market behaviour will be gathered either from secondary sources or from specially commissioned surveys carried out on behalf of the client. Some agencies are part of a group within which there is also a market research firm.

• **Planning.** To give specialist MARKETING advice to the "generalist" ACCOUNT DIRECTOR. In some agencies the planning department is merged with the research department.

- **CREATIVE.** The place where bright new advertising ideas are supposed to be fermented.
- **MEDIA.** Responsible for planning advertising schedules and for buying space in the media.
- **Production.** Concerned with the making of all material for television, film or radio, and for the production of ready-to-print press advertising material. Smaller agencies subcontract much of their production outside the firm, but most bigger agencies have their own fully fledged production departments.
- **Traffic.** This is sometimes called the control department. It is responsible for seeing that each stage of the production process is completed on schedule. The deadlines that the department follows are imposed by publication dates or by broadcast transmission times.
- **Accounts.** Similar to the accounts department in a commercial firm. It is responsible for BILLING clients, for buying media space, and for paying freelance artists, photographers and writers.

One agency's advice on how best to use an agency is as follows.

❐ Provide it with a clear and practical brief.
❐ Establish a clear and workable budget.
❐ Provide a realistic timetable.
❐ Carefully check the agency's copy, artwork, and so on.
❐ Have a clear and realistic business objective against which the agency's work can be measured.

Advertising agents top the list of those who misuse language on purpose, but it is their job to excite our emotions and atrophy our thoughts.
Sir Ernest Gowers

ADVERTISING BRIEF
A statement on the objectives of an ADVERTISING CAMPAIGN that is agreed between an ADVERTISING

AGENCY and its client (sometimes known as an "agency brief"). It contains a brief history of the PRODUCT to be advertised, and is the starting point for any agency's work.

A good brief helps to minimise misunderstanding in the delicate relationship between an agency and its client. In theory, the client determines the advertising objectives, plans the overall advertising strategy and sets the advertising budget. The agency then prepares and evaluates the advertisements and develops a MEDIA PLAN. In practice, however, the division of labour is determined largely by the nature of the relationship between agency and client.

ADVERTISING CAMPAIGN

A co-ordinated series of advertisements appearing over a defined period of time and in different MEDIA. An advertising campaign aims to obtain the maximum influence on a TARGET MARKET for a given amount of money. It is used most effectively for launching a new PRODUCT or relaunching an old one.

ADVERTISING STANDARDS

The potential for advertisers to put out material that is misleading, or even downright dishonest, is a continual problem for governments and regulatory authorities. The maintenance of high standards in ADVERTISING is usually left, first, to the advertising industry itself.

In most developed countries the industry sets out a code of behaviour which is rich in words like "legal", "decent", "honest" and "truthful". Behind them is the general principle that advertisements should not mislead, misrepresent or offend.

In many countries, film and television commercials are vetted by a regulatory authority before they are shown. Press advertising is, however, ultimately controlled by the ability of the public to complain about it. By definition, that almost always occurs after the event, in other words when the damage has been done.

Blatant cases of misleading advertising are rare

nowadays. However, occasional examples still creep through. In the USA the Federal Trade Commission judges whether advertising is unfair or deceptive. If it deems that it is, then the advertiser has to publish or broadcast "corrective advertising", and pay for it itself.

Complaints most often focus on the decency aspect of advertisements; Benetton has been a notorious offender. Advertisements promoting its range of women and children's wear have used a photograph of a man dying of AIDS, and of a nun affectionately kissing a monk.

When business is good it pays to advertise.
When business is bad you've got to advertise.
Anon

ADVERTISING/SALES RATIO
The total expenditure on ADVERTISING in a period expressed as a percentage of the total sales for the period. The A/S ratio can be applied to a BRAND, a company, or even a whole industry It is widely used as a yardstick for deciding on advertising budgets.

ADVERTORIAL
Most manufacturers believe that the best ADVERTISING in newspapers and magazines for their products is flattering copy in the editorial sections of the publication. More people make purchasing decisions on the basis of the prosaic recommendations of a well-respected correspondent than on the strength of a dazzlingly beautiful advertisement. A major part of the job of PUBLIC RELATIONS is to encourage such copy.

Failing that, some companies try to make their advertisements look like editorial. Publishers that are keener on revenue than integrity may allow such "advertorials" to appear in their publications but usually with the word "Advertisement" printed on the page.

AFFLUENT MATERIALIST
They used to be called the Jones's, the people that everyone felt under pressure to keep up with. Now affluent materialists are a category of consumer in a useful new classification of pan-European lifestyles (see LIFESTYLE).

AFTER-SALES SERVICE
A service provided by a manufacturer to a consumer after the consumer has bought the manufacturer's PRODUCT. After-sales service has been particularly significant in the MARKETING of consumer durables like washing machines, heating systems and personal computers. It includes regular checks, repairs, supplying spare parts, and so on. Such a service may be provided under the terms of a specific maintenance agreement (separate from the purchase) for which the consumer pays a regular fee.

As manufacturers become more QUALITY conscious, after-sales service becomes less important. Cars, for instance, need servicing much less frequently than they used to.

> *German brand names are rarely entertaining. But Agfa, perhaps, takes the prize for humourlessness. It is an abbreviation of Aktiengesellschaft für Anilinfabrikation: the limited company for dye manufacturing.*

AIDA
One of the oldest mnemonics in MARKETING, AIDA describes the stepping stones to successful communication:

- get Attention;
- hold Interest;
- arouse Desire; and
- obtain Action.

ALTERNATE DEMAND
A term taken from economics referring to the demand for products that can be substituted for each

other, for example: tea and coffee as drinks; buses and trains as transport; gas and electricity as heating fuel; magazines and television as home entertainment.

Marketers looking at the competition that exists for their products must look not only at manufacturers of similar products but also at the alternate demand.

The Alfa-Romeo car got its name because an Italian called Nicola Romeo was once manager of a company called Societá Anonima Lombarda Fabbrica Automobili. The car that Mr Romeo's company produced should (strictly) have been known as the Salfa-Romeo.

AMA
See below.

AMERICAN MARKETING ASSOCIATION
The leading association of MARKETING managers and teachers in the USA. Founded in 1936 the AMA has chapters all over the country and sponsors a number of annual conferences. It also publishes several journals with a wide international circulation. The oldest, the *Journal of Marketing*, dates back to the end of the nineteenth century.

Nothing works faster than Anadin ... so get nothing.
Anon

ANIMAL TESTING
The testing of household products or medicines on animals before the products are sold to humans. In some countries it is a legal requirement that certain potentially harmful substances be so tested before they can be consumed by homo sapiens.

Animal testing is on the decline. The activities of anti-vivisection groups and the success of companies (like Body Shop) which make a point of avoiding it, have persuaded even cosmetics giants like Revlon and Avon to stop testing on animals.

Alligators? Just floating handbags really.
Copywriter

ANIMATIC
The moving bits in a television advertisement; or a rough commercial made from a STORYBOARD.

A&P
Shorthand for the department responsible for AD-VERTISING and PROMOTION in a large corporation. Also the name of a pioneering US DEPARTMENT STORE, the Great Atlantic and Pacific Tea Company, the original coast-to-coast SUPERMARKET.

ATOMISTIC TEST
The separate testing of individual elements of the DESIGN of a new advertisement or PACKAGING. For example, in an advertisement for Levi's jeans the JINGLE might be tried out on an audience separately from the look of the male model wearing the jeans, or of the female model looking at the male model who is looking at the jeans, and so on. A "holistic test" tests all these elements together.

ATTITUDE
The collection of beliefs and feelings that together influence a consumer's buying behaviour. The factors that go towards determining attitudes are complex. MARKETING specialists try to understand them in order to present products in a favourable light, or to try and change attitudes through so-called "attitude management".

When Honda first decided to introduce its motorcycles into the US the company was faced with a hostile attitude to the PRODUCT: motorcycles were seen as dangerous and associated with violent gangs. However, with ADVERTISING based on the slogan "You meet the nicest people on a Honda", the Japanese company succeeded in changing attitudes to the motorcycle.

ATTRIBUTES
The characteristics of a PRODUCT that are important to consumers. For example, aroma, flavour, caffeine content and price are the main attributes of instant coffee; flavour, COLOUR, smell, thickness, saltiness and texture are the attributes of chicken broth.

Different consumers weigh the importance of a product's attributes differently, particularly consumers living in different regions. Thick and chunky chicken soup may be popular with the British, but the French prefer to drink their chicken soup clear and thin.

Part of the marketer's skill is to communicate to each group of consumers the attributes that most appeal to it.

AUDIENCE RESEARCH
The process of measuring and analysing radio and television audiences. The size and composition of such audiences are basic bread-and-butter information for MARKETING managers and ADVERTISING AGENCIES. So too are the circulation figures of newspapers and magazines (see AUDIT BUREAU OF CIRCULATION).

AUDIT
A survey of the sales of a PRODUCT, at different retail outlets, by price, size, and so on. Such surveys are carried out by a number of research companies (the most famous is A.C. NIELSEN), and are often commissioned by a syndicate of manufacturers in the same industrial sector. The data gathered usually covers a one-month period.

The development of EPOS and laser scanning has improved the ability of researchers to produce ever sophisticated audits.

AUDIT BUREAU OF CIRCULATION
Many countries around the world have a national organisation with this name. Commonly known as ABC, the Audit Bureau of Circulation publishes regular audited statements of newspapers' and magazines' circulation figures. These are eagerly analysed by advertisers who need to know how

many readers they are reaching, and at what cost
(see COST PER MILLE).

In the United States ABC is sponsored by national and local advertisers, as well as by ADVERTIS-
ING agencies and publishers. In the UK, too, most
newspaper and magazine publishers belong to it.

AUTOMAT

A vending machine that sells goods automatically.
The goods on sale are displayed through glass or
perspex windows, and consumers make a series
of choices by pressing different buttons. They
then insert the necessary payment and the goods
are released.

AUTOMATIC MERCHANDISING

The selling of goods through an AUTOMAT, a
method in which only one human hand (the consumer's) is involved. Automatic merchandising is
particularly appropriate in locations where there is
a heavy round-the-clock stream of human traffic-
like railway stations, airports, or the lobbies of big
office blocks. It is also suited for particular products: cigarettes and soft drinks account for about
70% of all automatic merchandising.

AWARENESS

The ability of individuals to remember a particular
advertisement. Awareness is measured in two ways.

1 Prompted. The individual is asked a question
like: "Have you heard of an instant coffee called
Maxwell House?"
2 Unprompted (or spontaneous). The individual is asked a question like: "Can you name a
BRAND of instant coffee?"

Measures of awareness are widely used as indica-
tors of the effectiveness of MARKETING strategies.

BABY BOOMERS

The generation of consumers born in the years immediately after the second world war when, in most developed countries, there was a pronounced upward blip in the birth rate. Born when times were hard but optimistic, baby boomers have been studied closely by marketers on account of their numbers and their purchasing power.

In the 1970s the baby boomers themselves gave birth to another blip in the population as they had children of their own.

Many are now becoming EMPTY NESTERS.

BAIT AND SWITCH

A MARKETING practice that has been outlawed in the USA. A RETAILER (or advertiser) "baits" customers into wanting to purchase something (by, say, offering it very cheaply) but then makes them "switch" their purchase (to a more profitable item). Customers are persuaded to switch because, for example, retailers say that they have run out of the advertised product (which they had no intention of selling in the first place).

BANDED PACK

A sales PROMOTION device similar to a QUANTITY DISCOUNT. Two or more items of the same PRODUCT are bound together as a single pack; they are then offered for sale at a price that is less than the combined price of the items sold singly.

Banded packs include familiar offers like "Three for the price of two", or "Buy two and get a third free". They are frequently used for selling items such as bars of soap or toothpaste. But even airlines occasionally sell banded packs: "Fly first-class to Miami and bring a friend for free."

BAR CODE

A series of lines of varying thickness printed on the side of a PRODUCT or its label. Bar coding is now familiar in many countries, and allows an electronic scanner at the POINT OF SALE to read automatically certain information about the product (like its price). This speeds up the checkout process while at the same time allowing vendors to keep a tighter control on their inventory and to see new patterns in their sales.

The European bar code consists of 13 digits. The first two identify the country issuing the code; the next five give the manufacturer's number; and the next five show the product item numbers, which are allocated by the manufacturer to the RETAILER. The last digit is a "check" digit, used by the computer to guard against misreading.

Retailers can use the five digits allocated to them by the manufacturer to store information about their products, including the price. These digits can then be used to provide customers with fully itemised printed bills at electronic checkout counters.

In the USA bar codes are referred to as "universal product coding", but this is a misnomer. The US system is not being used universally, although there are attempts to standardise bar coding worldwide.

After the second world war both the Americans and the British were offered the Volkswagen "Beetle" design by the Germans. The UK's Lord Rootes said: "To build the car commercially would be a completely uneconomic enterprise." The Americans were even more blunt. One senior executive said to his boss: "Mr Ford, I don't think what we are being offered here is worth a damn." The Beetle went on to become one of the most successful car designs of all time.

BARGAIN BASEMENT
This used to refer to the basement of a DEPARTMENT STORE where merchandise was traditionally sold off at discounted prices. Department stores find other uses for their basements these days, but the expression still continues, as in "bargain-basement prices".

BELONGER
One category in a well-known US classification of consumers (see LIFESTYLE).

BELOW-THE-LINE
Any promotional activity other than ADVERTISING in the MEDIA. See also ABOVE-THE-LINE.

BENEFIT SEGMENTATION
The division of a MARKET into groups of consumers who are looking for the same benefit from a PRODUCT. For example, one segment of the toothpaste market consists of those who are chiefly concerned with preventing tooth decay; another contains all those consumers whose primary concern is the whiteness and brightness of their teeth.

BIG TICKET
The sort of big purchase that consumers often make on credit; for example, of cars or washing machines. The MARKETING of such items demands greater emphasis on ancillary services, such as credit terms, AFTER-SALES SERVICE, guarantees, and so on.

BILLBOARD
Literally, boards on which to stick bills (that is, advertisements – as in "bill of fare") Billboards are usually large, visible and close to major roads and highways. They are also known as hoardings.

In some countries billboards are strictly controlled by law; in others the controls are lax, especially (as is often the case) when the billboards are owned by local governments.

I think that I shall never see
A billboard lovely as a tree.
Indeed unless the billboards fall
I'll never see a tree at all.
Ogden Nash

BILLING
A measure of the size of an ADVERTISING AGENCY. Generally, agencies are paid a percentage of the amount that it costs to put their clients' advertisements in the MEDIA. This cost is called the advertiser's "billing", and gives a rough guide to the amount of business that an agency is getting.

B

BILL POSTER
Also known as bill sticker. A person who sticks "bills" (small printed advertisements) on to spare urban walls or BILLBOARDS. Unoccupied retail premises are vulnerable to bill posters and often post their own bill declaring that "Bill Posters will be Prosecuted".

Bill Posters is Innocent.
Graffiti

BIODEGRADABLE
The ability of a PRODUCT to be broken down "naturally", that is by the forces of nature. Leave a biodegradable product in the ground for some time and it will not exist in any recognisable form.

In today's environmentally conscious MARKETING, biodegradable is a valuable attribute of a BRAND. Consumers feel good about buying biodegradable PACKAGING, for example.

Birds Eye, the frozen foods, were named after a Mr Birdseye. Clarence (known as "Bob") Birdseye (1886–1956) invented a process for freezing food in small enough packages for it to be sold retail. The idea came to him on a trip to the Arctic.

BLIND ENVELOPE
An envelope enclosing a MAILSHOT which does not have a transparent window through which to read an address.

Biro sounds like a perfect brand name. In fact it is the name of the inventor of the quick-drying, non-blobbing pen. Laszlo Biro was a Hungarian who fled from the Nazis to Argentina. There he first patented the pen that is named after him.

BLIND TEST
A MARKET-RESEARCH technique in which two unidentified products are sampled by consumers

---

who indicate their preference. Blind testing is often used in new PRODUCT research to test the product against an established BRAND.

Because brand names and PACKAGING heavily influence consumers' PERCEPTION of products, blind testing is the only way to measure factors such as taste, smell and texture on a comparative basis.

BLISTER PACK
A form of PACKAGING in which products are wrapped in clear plastic (or with a clear transparent "window") so that consumers can properly see what they are buying before they buy it.

BLOW-UP
A greatly enlarged photograph used in a MARKETING presentation, made famous by a fashionable film of the 1960s with the same name. It is not greatly different from a "Beauty Shot": a close-up picture of a PRODUCT.

BLURB
The short piece of copy that appears on the jacket or inside cover of a book. Hence any short piece of copy that praises something extravagantly.

Look how glamorous acronyms can become when divorced from their original connotations. BMW stands for Bayerische Motoren Werke: the Bavarian Motor Works.

BODY COPY
The main text in a piece of MARKETING material, as opposed to the headlines or the details in footnotes.

BODY LANGUAGE
A means of non-verbal communication expressed through movements of the body. Much television ADVERTISING uses body language to express emotions: it is quicker and easier than using words. It is also more universal. Much body language is common to peoples in the East, the West, the

North and the South. But there are crucial differences: for example, nodding the head up and down means "yes" in some cultures, and "no" in others.

BRAND

According to Philip Kotler, author of *Marketing Management*, the world's standard MARKETING textbook, a brand is:

A name, term, symbol or design (or a combination of them) which is intended to signify the goods or services of one seller or group of sellers and to differentiate them from those of competitors.

When marketed successfully a brand becomes a powerful force. Nike, Mars, Virgin, Levi, for example, instantly identify products and services familiar to everyone. In markets where famous brands exist, competitors are always at a disadvantage.

Brands may be used in different ways.

● Family brands are PRODUCT names which all contain the name of the company: Heinz Tomato Ketchup, Heinz Baked Beans, and so on; Cadbury's Fruit and Nut, Cadbury's Smash, and so on.
● Individual brands stand alone. Procter & Gamble's products all carry individual brand names, for instance, Ariel, Flash, Pampers.
● Some companies use a different brand name for a different PRODUCT LINE: Sears Roebuck, for example, sells appliances under the brand name Kenmore and tools under the brand name Craftsman.
● Sometimes the brand name is attached to a company or divisional name (as when United Biscuits launched "McVitie's Hob-nobs"). This is known as an umbrella brand, and is used to endorse the product while at the same time allowing it to develop its own brand personality.
● Brands can also be owned by middlemen (see DEALER BRAND) or by manufacturers (see MANUFACTURER BRAND).
● Brands can be people as well as things.

Madonna is a brand; so is Tom Cruise; and so (to her eternal bemusement) was Marilyn Monroe.

The word "brand" has been around for a long time. It is derived from an old Norse word *brandr* which means to burn; hence the "branding" of livestock.

> *Marketing guys would love the Jolly Green Giant to get brown around the edges, so that they could launch a new brand.*
>
> Anon

BRAND IMAGE

The aura behind a particular BRAND. In his book *World Class Brands* Chris Macrae developed a typology of brands. In it there are six main categories.

1 The ritual brand. Associated with special occasions, such as champagne for a wedding, cranberry sauce for a Thanksgiving dinner.

2 The symbol brand. For example, the famous Lacoste alligator or Louis Vuitton's LV monogram. The symbol is the value; what it is attached to is almost irrelevant.

3 The "heritage of good" brand. This is usually the first brand to establish itself as providing specific benefits: Kellogg's for a "bright start to the day"; The Body Shop for "how to have an environmentally clean conscience, painless feet and no wrinkles".

4 The aloof snob brand. Ferraris, American Express Platinum cards, and so on. For the rich who, despite what Scott Fitzgerald said, still feel the need to emphasise that they are different.

5 Belonging brands. These give the consumer a feeling of belonging to a group. For example, Marlboro smokers, who are all macho cowboys at heart (although when Marlboro was first launched they were all smart city women); or wearers of Benetton clothes, who are all members of a multi-racial, multicoloured global village.

6 The legend. For example, the Levi 501 jean (the first ever made by the company) or the Porsche Carrera, in an early model of which James Dean, the moody-young-man "brand" of the 1950s, crashed and died.

BRAND LOYALTY

The aim of all "brand managers" is to secure the sustained loyalty of consumers to their particular PRODUCT. Brand loyalty comes about through consumers' continuing satisfaction with the product, and through effective and often heavy PROMOTION. Strong brand loyalty reduces the impact of ADVERTISING by competitive brands, and discourages brand switching.

> *Petrol retailers should recognise that they are not selling a product but offering a branded experience.*
> Gérard Lecoeur, design consultant

BRAND MANAGEMENT

Also known as product management. A management system developed in the 1930s by Procter & Gamble, it has grown into a widely accepted method of managing individual brands in multiproduct companies.

A BRAND manager is given responsibility for a single brand, and becomes that PRODUCT's champion and enthusiast within the company. He or she sets the brand's MARKETING objectives, plans what action is needed to achieve these objectives (such as TARGET MARKET identification, ADVERTISING, sales PROMOTION, PACKAGING, and so on), schedules and co-ordinates all the marketing activities, and reports to the product group management.

Most companies using this P&G system of brand management treat the brand manager's domain as a PROFIT CENTRE.

BRAND STRETCHING

The idea that one brand name can be stretched

across a large number of products and/or services. Brand stretching is widely believed to have limitations. If, for example, the quality of one of the products or services in the brand portfolio slips, the image of the others in it may suffer.

> *"Each time Virgin entered a new business all the conventional pundits whined that we were stretching our brand too far. Rather than worrying too much about brands being stretched too far, people will have to stretch their imaginations further."*
>
> Richard Branson

BRAND VALUATION

The process of attaching a value in a company's balance sheet to its brands. That these brands have considerable value is beyond question. When Philip Morris bought the Kraft food company in 1988 it paid $12.9 billion. That was four times the value of Kraft's tangible assets; in other words Philip Morris paid just short of $10 billion for intangible assets. Most of them were the brands that Kraft had developed over the years: its own-name range of products plus things like Miracle Whip and Breyers ice-cream.

This, and similar purchases at about the same time, alerted companies to the fact that their brands might be a significant intangible asset, and they started to put figures on them in their balance sheets.

How do you work out what these numbers should be? A firm called Interbrand has developed one formula for calculating BRAND values. It takes an objective measure of the brand's recent profitability, and multiplies it by a number (up to 20) based on a subjective judgment of the following seven aspects of the brand.

- Its leadership (or otherwise) in its market.
- Its stability (or longevity).
- The nature of the market: is it large and stable (like food and drink) or subject to fast-changing

fashion (like green hair-dye)?

● Its internationality: international brands are assumed to have more strength (both domestically and abroad) than purely national brands.
● The trend for the brand.
● The marketing support for the brand.
● Its protection in law: as a registered trademark, and so on.

Brillo – the UK kitchen scouring pad – is short for the very British "Brilliant-o", as in "Brasso" (which is of the same vintage). In Italian brillo *means "sozzled".*

BROWN GOODS

Consumer durables that used to be encased in brown veneer, such as old-fashioned radios, televisions in cabinets, and gramophones. Brown goods were usually contrasted with WHITE GOODS.

Nowadays white goods are still by and large encased in white, but brown goods are more often wrapped in black, or in shades of grey. Hence the expression "brown goods" has fallen into disuse.

BUNDLING

The process of offering services that are related to a PRODUCT at a special price to those who purchase the product. For example, software packages are often bundled with the purchase of computer hardware. Banks bundle free chequing accounts or free safe deposit services to those who maintain high average balances in their accounts.

BURST

See DRIP CAMPAIGN.

BUSINESS-TO-BUSINESS ADVERTISING

Sometimes called industrial advertising. The majority of ADVERTISING is directed at individual consumers, but there is a significant segment that is produced by businesses for businesses: manufacturers of machine tools or construction equipment do not market their products to individuals; they market them to other companies.

Specialist trade journals and trade fairs are important MEDIA for these companies, and for business-to-business advertising in general. (In the USA there are almost three times as many specialist trade journals as consumer magazines.)

BUYER'S MARKET

Any MARKET in which supply exceeds demand. Such a market can arise either because the supply of a PRODUCT has been increased by a number of new entrants into the market; or because the demand for the product has declined as recession or changing consumer tastes have hit the market. Either way, buyers will force down prices in such a market until supply is cut by a reduction in the number of suppliers.

BUYGRID

A widely used model of industrial buying which identifies three different types of situation.

1 New task. The situation that occurs when an organisation has no previous experience of the task in hand.

2 Modified rebuy. The situation in which an organisation reassesses its position, perhaps searching for QUALITY improvements and cost reductions. Such a reassessment is usually triggered by some dissatisfaction with existing suppliers.

3 Straight rebuy. The situation that requires little reassessment, and largely entails reordering from current suppliers.

BUYING CYCLE

The frequency with which products are purchased. The buying cycle for bread is a matter of days; for sugar a matter of weeks; and for cars a matter of years (and rising).

CALL CENTRE

A place where a number of people are gathered together to take telephone enquiries and orders from customers and potential customers. Call centres have grown rapidly in recent years with the growth of DIRECT MARKETING. Many of them are at the end of TOLL-FREE NUMBERS which allow customers to call at almost any time of the day or night in order to make purchases or enquiries.

The increasing sophistication of telecommunications means that the people who answer the phones may not be all physically gathered together in one place. They can answer calls in their own homes where they can be linked not only to the call centre's common telephone number (or numbers) but also to its computer database.

Some computers can identify the source of a call before it is answered. So operators can then have all the customer's details called up on to their computer screen before the operator has had time to pick up the phone.

CANNIBALISATION

When increased sales of one BRAND result in decreased sales of another within the same PRODUCT LINE. Cannibalisation is a danger when products or brands in a company's product line are insufficiently differentiated; or when competition among a company's brand managers becomes too intense (see BRAND MANAGEMENT).

There is always a risk of cannibalisation when a company extends a product line. For example, when powder-based detergents were first marketed in liquid form there was a danger that the extension brand (the liquid detergent) would reduce sales of the original powdered brand to such an extent that the combined sales (of powder and liquid) were less than the sales of the original powder on its own.

CAPTIVE MARKET

A group of consumers that has no choice. This may be either because products (or services) are provided by a monopoly supplier (like telecoms services in most countries), or because the consumers are in a particular situation which does not allow them choice. For example, travellers by train or plane can only have the food and drink that the transport company decides to make available to them.

Caran d'Ache, the famous make of Swiss pencils, are named after a French illustrator, Emmanuel Poire, who used the name Caran d'Ache as a nom de plume. He took the name from the Russian word karandash, *which means pencil.*

CASCADING

A MARKETING strategy, favoured by the Japanese, in which a small well-defined MARKET segment is penetrated first before the manufacturer "cascades" into other markets. For example, Honda started in the USA with the marketing of small motorcycles; it is now a major importer of automobiles into the American market.

The benefit of such a strategy is that an initial entry into a narrowly focused market provokes little competition. That enables the marketer to build up a DISTRIBUTION and servicing network without attracting too much attention.

CASH AND CARRY

A form of limited-service wholesaling that has become popular in various sectors in the USA and the UK. Cash-and-carry shops are like wholesale warehouses (taking delivery in bulk from manufacturers).

The RETAILER or customer gets a minimal service. There is no sales force, no delivery service, no credit, no reordering assistance; in short, no frills. The retailer or customer goes to the warehouse, pays for the goods, and takes them away. It means lower costs to the WHOLESALER and lower prices to the retailer.

The success of the cash-and-carry concept owed much to changing patterns of consumer shopping. As shoppers turned more and more to huge SUPERMARKET chains, the only way that smaller independent retailers (like corner groceries or village stores) could compete was by cutting costs to the bone. That included buying their stock from the cash-and-carry chains. Small hotels and restaurants also rely heavily on cash-and-carry outlets.

CATALOGUE STORE
Such a store combines the benefits of catalogue selling with those of the BARGAIN BASEMENT. It deals in well-known products like jewellery, appliances, luggage, watches and hi-fi equipment. Customers who call at the store view the goods in locked glass cases, and then order them from catalogues. The inventory is stored behind the catalogue showroom, and customers' orders are brought out to them. Customer comfort is not a first priority: lines may form both for ordering and for collecting goods. Prices, however, are discounted and are very competitive.

CATI
See COMPUTER-ASSISTED TELEPHONE INTERVIEWING.

CAVEAT EMPTOR
Latin for "let the buyer beware", a phrase of great legal significance in the days before the spate of modern laws designed to protect the consumer. In the absence of an express GUARANTEE in a contract, buyers purchased goods at their own risk.

Today's consumers are protected by laws both in respect of the manufacture of products (through warranties) and in respect of the retailing of them. In the UK, for example, goods bought from retailers must correspond with their description (be what they are said to be). They must also be of "merchantable QUALITY" and be fit for their purpose (do what they are meant to do).

CENTRAL BUYING
Each outlet in DEPARTMENT STORE or SUPERMARKET chains does not do its own buying of merchandise. Buying is done centrally at a head office, and

the merchandise is distributed by the head office around the chain.

Such central buying is done in order to make economies of scale: the head office can get bigger discounts for buying in greater bulk, and it requires fewer people to do the same amount of buying.

CHAIN STORE

A shop belonging to a group of retail outlets that are linked in one of three possible ways.

1 Corporate chains. These consist of retail outlets that are owned and managed by one company. The chains have a central buying office and centrally managed MARKETING, ADVERTISING and MERCHANDISING.

The corporate chain was pioneered by F.W. Woolworth, which opened its first store in the USA in 1879. Nowadays the grocery business is increasingly dominated by chain stores such as Sainsbury and Tesco in the UK, and Safeway and Walmart in the USA.

2 Voluntary association chains. These are groups of independent retailers who gather themselves around a single WHOLESALER.

3 Franchises. The fastest-growing retail chains in many countries in recent years have been FRANCHISE operations like McDonald's, Benetton, Pizza Hut, and so on.

Many products have been named after Lord Chesterfield, a 19th-century symbol of gracious living: the Chesterfield sofa, the Chesterfield coat and the Chesterfield cigarette.

CHANNEL CAPTAIN

Whoever is the most powerful member of the channel of DISTRIBUTION (from manufacturer to WHOLESALER to RETAILER) is known as the channel captain. Traditionally, the channel captain has been a manufacturer. In the car industry, companies like General Motors and Renault have totally dominated their dealer networks.

But there have also been retailers who have been channel captains. In the USA, The Limited built up such a position for itself in a very short space of time. It has its own manufacturers to feed its 3,800 stores, and it controls a bank which provides credit to divisions within the company as well as credit cards to its customers. Marks and Spencer occupies a similar position in the UK.

CHANNEL CONFLICT

Disagreement between members of a DISTRIBUTION CHANNEL. Such conflict can be either horizontal or vertical.

- Horizontal channel conflict occurs among retailers when one RETAILER feels that another is competing too strongly, or is invading its territory unacceptably with its ADVERTISING.
- Vertical channel conflict occurs between retailers and their suppliers (manufacturers) when either side feels itself unduly dominated by the other.

When Chrysler introduced a new car into the Mexican market called the Nova it forgot that in Mexico no va means "it does not go".

CHARTERED INSTITUTE OF MARKETING

Founded in the UK in 1911, the Chartered Institute of Marketing (CIM) is now Europe's largest professional body for MARKETING and sales practitioners. It has some 25,000 members and over 7,000 registered students from around the world. Its certificate and diploma qualifications are widely recognised, and its marketing training department is one of the largest in Europe.

CHERRY PICKING

The act of choosing/buying only special offers or LOSS-LEADERS. This rather defeats the purpose of the special offer, which is to persuade a customer who is enticed by it to purchase lots of things which are fully priced and carrying a handsome margin.

Cherry picking also refers to a practice found among companies entering new markets. The company attempts to pick off only the best customers for its business – for example, a bank that looks to provide services only to companies and individuals with the very highest credit ratings.

Cinzano is one of the oldest names in business. As long ago as 1757, Carlo Stefano Cinzano and Giovanni Giacomo Cinzano were distilling the beverage that bears their name in a factory near Turin.

CIRCULATION AND READERSHIP

Circulation is the average number of people who read each issue of a newspaper or magazine; it is a number closely watched by advertisers who want to reach a certain size of audience, and it is audited (to make sure that publishers do not cheat) by organisations like the AUDIT BUREAU OF CIRCULATION.

Readership is a slightly different concept. It is the number of individuals who read each copy of a publication. Whereas something like a cheap local daily newspaper will be read by only one person (the purchaser), more expensive and longer-lasting magazines will be read over their lifetime by several people (especially if they are left in the waiting rooms of badly organised dentists).

The total number of people who read a publication is the circulation multiplied by the readership. That is unlikely to be the same as the number of people who notice the advertisements inside the publication.

CLASSIFIED ADVERTISEMENT

Small advertisements of a few lines, written without professional help, that appear in serried ranks in certain newspapers and magazines. They are often ADVERTISING homes or second-hand household goods for sale; and increasingly they are offering deeply discounted broken hearts.

C

Each classified advertisement is relatively cheap, but added together they can become a significant source of revenue for a publication. In the UK, *The Lady* magazine has thrived for the best part of a century on classified advertising for nannies, home helps and au pairs.

CLUSTER ANALYSIS
A statistical technique that sorts a SAMPLE into a number of groups (or clusters) that have features in common.

Coca-Cola, the most famous brand name in the world, was formed in 1886 out of the names of two of its ingredients: extract of coca leaves, and cola nuts. The coca leaf is also the source of cocaine, but it is no longer used in the manufacture of Coca-Cola. Both, though, are still known as Coke. And so is anthracite.

COGNITIVE DISSONANCE
The dissatisfaction that occurs when there is a difference between a consumer's EXPECTATIONS of a PRODUCT and the product's performance. Since consumers' expectations about products are largely created by ADVERTISING, this dissonance may be reduced by only making claims that are consistent with a product's performance.

Offers of guarantees, warranties and AFTER-SALES SERVICE can reassure consumers that any source of dissatisfaction will be put to rights. They reduce consumers' expectations of cognitive dissonance.

COLD CALLING
Calling on a customer without a prior appointment. Many retail businesses expect sales people to drop in regularly and unexpectedly. For many kinds of selling, however, cold calling is unwelcome, inefficient and time-wasting. Where it is unavoidable, the hit rate (that is, the inverse of the number of calls that have to be made before a customer makes a purchase) is very low.

COLLARETTE
A cardboard collar around the neck of a bottle that carries an advertisement or a sales PROMOTION.

COLOUR
The power of colour in establishing a BRAND should not be underestimated. Different colours mean different things: red is universally considered to be warm; blue is generally cold. But the significance of colours is also culturally determined. Certain yellows and oranges that the Japanese appreciate, for example, do not go down well in Europe.

A PRODUCT'S colour can become a valuable asset. *The Economist*'s red is recognisable on a BILLBOARD without any words; Marlboro's red is a named colour in many a printer's spectrum. The strength of a PROMOTION may be greatly diminished if a printer does not reproduce the precise colour associated with a brand.

COMFORTABLE BELONGER
A species of consumer found in great abundance in Europe (see LIFESTYLE).

Communication takes place in the ear of the listener, not in the mouth of the speaker.
Anon

COMMUNICATIONS STRATEGY
The choice of different ways in which marketers set out to communicate with their markets: inevitably a combination of direct face-to-face communication between a SALES PERSON and a potential customer, and indirect non-personal communication through ADVERTISING and sales PROMOTION.

The nature of a PRODUCT and of its MARKET influences a company's communications strategy. If its products are targeted at mass consumer markets, and if the company can afford it, then its communications strategy need consist of nothing more than a strong dose of MEDIA advertising.

On the other hand, industrial MARKETING generally calls for personal selling to meet the often highly specialised needs of industrial customers.

Communications is the most important form of marketing.
Akio Morita

COMPARATIVE ADVERTISING

The controversial practice of ADVERTISING a PRODUCT by comparing it – to its advantage – with its competitors. This goes beyond the old practice of comparing the advertiser's product with an (anonymous) Brand X. All brands are named.

Comparative advertising can be very effective, but it is potentially litigious. One unsupported bit of knocking copy about the competition, and the law suits can fall as fast as the sales chart.

COMPETITION

A contest (as distinct from a PRIZE DRAW) run by a manufacturer with prizes designed to entice customers to try the manufacturer's product. If it's part of the launch of a new ice-cream, for example, the competition prize might be a visit to a Disney theme park. In order to avoid being a lottery (and thus to avoid being subject to tight regulatory scrutiny) a competition must involve an element of skill – guessing what city a photograph depicts, for example.

In order to avoid splitting the prize into many parts (difficult to do with a weekend at Disney World), the compilers of competitions frequently ask for entrants to finish a sentence such as "I love Sudsy best because it is…" They can then choose a single winner since no two sentences will be the same.

COMPUTER-ASSISTED TELEPHONE INTERVIEWING

Computer-assisted telephone interviewing (CATI) is conducted by an interviewer using a computer and a computerised QUESTIONNAIRE. The interviewer reads the questions from the computer's visual display unit and keys in the respondents' answers.

Since the computer can follow complex questionnaire routing very efficiently (for example, "If the answer to Question 10 is No, then go to Question 15"), interviewer errors are much reduced. The processing of data is also very much faster.

CONCENTRATED SEGMENTATION

Some companies identify a comparatively small segment of a MARKET on which to concentrate their MARKETING effort. By selecting such a niche they hope to avoid head-on competition with larger and more powerful rivals.

A classic example of a successful PRODUCT in a small market is the Rolls-Royce car, which has catered for many years to a small but affluent international clientele. Another is provided by a California company which found a niche for itself making personalised coaches for rock stars, people who spend much of their lives literally "on the road".

Concentrated segmentation has become better known as "niche marketing". Mass marketers will only ignore niches for as long as they see no way to compete in them profitably, and they do not feel threatened by them. IBM, for example, entered the downmarket cheap personal computer market (under another BRAND name) because the threat to its personal-computer business from a vast range of copy-cat cut-price manufacturers became too great even for Big Blue to ignore.

CONCEPT TESTING

A technique used to test new ideas (concepts) at an early stage in the development of a PRODUCT. QUALITATIVE RESEARCH techniques, such as GROUP DISCUSSION, can yield valuable insights into how consumers might perceive a new product idea, how it might be used, when, and by whom. For example, a group of housewives might be brought together and asked to test the concept of robotic housekeeping.

CONCESSION

The right given to a RETAILER to sell from a certain

(usually small) space in a DEPARTMENT STORE, hotel or office block.

CONJOINT ANALYSIS

A technique used in NEW PRODUCT DEVELOPMENT. A company that wants to introduce a new product has to decide what particular features and qualities to give the product so that it can be properly positioned with respect to its competitors.

Every product has a large number of ATTRIBUTES: some of them (and some combinations of them) are more important than others. Conjoint analysis is a technique for testing the strength of the various combinations of features in order to develop a picture of the combination that is best liked by consumers.

The skill in conjoint analysis lies in choosing the right combinations. It is no good simply throwing together the most popular attributes. For example, suppose a company is designing a new ice-cream. It finds that all elderly people want soft ice-cream (and plain flavours) while all young people want candy-floss flavours and hard ice-cream. If it comes out with a soft candy-floss brand, it should not be surprised to find that nobody buys it.

In a consumer society there are inevitably two kinds of slaves: the prisoners of addiction and the prisoners of envy.
Ivan Illich

CONSUMER CREDIT

The granting of credit to individuals for the purchase of consumer goods and services. The too rapid withdrawal of consumer credit (either by an increase in interest rates, or by rationing, which governments have on occasion undertaken) can throw an economy into recession, so dependent are western consumers nowadays on the supply of credit.

In the MARKETING of consumer durables in particular, the provision of credit is a crucial element in securing a sale, and often a crucial element in the profitability of the manufacturer too. Some consumer goods manufacturers make more profit from financing sales than they do from the sales themselves.

CONSUMER PANEL
See DIARY PANEL.

CONSUMER PROFILE
A description of the age, social class, and other characteristics of consumers of a given PRODUCT or BRAND. Drawing up consumer profiles is an essential part of the development of a COMMUNICATIONS STRATEGY and of MARKET SEGMENTATION.

Des qualités trop supérieures rendent souvent un homme moins propre à la société. On ne va pas au marché avec des ingots; on y va avec de l'argent ou de la petite monnaie.

(Qualities too elevated often make a man unfit for society. We do not take ingots with us to market; we take silver or small change.)
Nicholas-Sebastien Chamfort (1741–94)

CONSUMER PROTECTION
Ways in which consumers are protected from sharp, illegal or dangerous practices by manufacturers. Much consumer protection legislation arose as a result of the CONSUMERISM movement in the USA and Europe in the 1960s.

There are several agencies in the USA that are involved in consumer protection and that have to be taken into account by companies planning to MARKET a PRODUCT in that country. They include the Federal Trade Commission, the Food and Drug Administration (FDA), the Consumer Products Safety Commission, the Environmental Protection Agency and the Office of Consumer Affairs.

In both the USA and the UK there are magazines produced by independent consumer associations in which products are tested and commented upon. In the USA the magazine is called *Consumer Reports*; in the UK *Which?* Both have a powerful influence on consumer behaviour.

CONSUMERISM

In 1962, the president of the USA, John F. Kennedy, issued a Consumers' Bill of Rights. It never became law, but it triggered a consumer "movement" for the rest of the decade, based on its recognition of the consumer's four basic rights.

1 The right to safety.
2 The right to be informed.
3 The right to choose.
4 The right to be heard.

The birth of consumerism marked a swing away from the overwhelming power of manufacturers, advertisers and retailers. It acknowledged that the level of material wealth in most parts of the USA and Europe was so high that consumers could choose which products to buy, or indeed whether to buy any. Societies were beyond the stage where almost anything that could be produced could be sold.

In some respects the Japanese economic miracle was based on an early recognition by Japanese firms of the consumer's new-found power. They recognised that such power would force manufacturers to be much more conscious of QUALITY and price.

Consumerism also marked a switch in the importance of different management disciplines. MARKETING became a crucial skill; gone was the almost total management preoccupation with the efficiency of the production process, and with such things as ergonomics and operations research.

The most famous champion of the consumer's cause was RALPH NADER who began his campaigns in the USA with his pursuit of General Motors and its "unsafe at any speed" Corvair car. His campaign led to the enactment of the Traffic and Motor Vehicle Safety Act.

CONTROL

A standard by which other production is measured. For example, quality control is the maintenance of quality at or above a certain required minimum control level.

In DIRECT MAIL a "control" is a standard response to a MAILSHOT, against which a new mailshot is measured. Thus a researcher can measure the impact of small changes in the copy inside a mailshot, or in the neighbourhood to which it is sent.

CONTROLLED CIRCULATION

When a publication is sent free to a number of targeted readers it is said to have a controlled circulation. The publication can tell potential advertisers that they will be reaching a particularly desirable audience (for them). On the other hand there is evidence to suggest that publications received free (and without being solicited) are not read anything like as thoroughly as those that are paid for.

CONVENIENCE STORE

Retail outlets, commonly known as C-Stores, that trade primarily on the appeal of the convenience that they offer to customers. (Convenience is one of the few weapons that small shops have with which to fight back against the increasing concentration of food retailing in the hands of big supermarkets.)

C-Stores have three competitive advantages.

1 They sell products based on a knowledge of local consumer needs.
2 They are open for long hours.
3 They are located near their customers.

In large cities convenience stores tend to be run by recent immigrants – Koreans in New York, Asians in London – because well-established residents are less prepared to put in the long and often tedious working hours required.

However, C-Stores are not confined to single-unit independent outlets. 7-Eleven, the successful

US chain of convenience stores, has thousands of outlets both inside and outside the USA.

COPYRIGHT

The legal protection given to artistic, literary, dramatic and musical works to prevent them from being copied without their creator's agreement. In general such protection lasts for the lifetime of the creator and for 50 years after his or her death.

Copyright also protects things like distinctive logo designs and ADVERTISING material. It has been included in the international effort to provide greater protection around the world to intellectual property rights. The Berne Convention (set up in 1886) also supposedly gives protection in those countries that have signed it. But it has no teeth to punish wrongdoers, and no system to arbitrate in disputes.

CORPORATE IDENTITY

The unique characteristics of a corporation together define its identity. These characteristics include obvious things like the DESIGN of its offices and the style of its PACKAGING as well as less tangible things like its beliefs and the way it conducts its business.

> *Corporate identity tells the world – whether actively or by default – just what the corporate strategy is.*
> Wally Olins

CORPORATE LOGO

A company's emblems, and a powerful part of its CORPORATE IDENTITY. Logos can become as familiar and as powerful as BRAND names. When AT&T, the USA's former telecommunications monopoly, was forcibly broken up, the courts decided that none of the resulting new companies had the right to use AT&T's logo, a distinctive emblem of a Bell telephone. The logo was withdrawn from use.

CORPORATE CAMPAIGN

An ADVERTISING CAMPAIGN that is aimed less at selling a particular PRODUCT or service of a company and more at propagating the good name and image of the company in general.

COST PER MILLE

Also expressed as cost per thousand (CPT). Cost per mille (CPM) is a convenient way of comparing the effectiveness of different MEDIA by calculating how much it costs, using each medium, to reach an audience of 1,000 people.

For magazines and newspapers the CPM is easy to calculate: if the cost of a full-page advertisement in a particular magazine is $10,000 and the circulation of the magazine is 250,000, then the CPM is $10,000 \div 250 = \$40$. For television it is not so simple; both the cost and the size of the audience depend on the time that the advertisement is shown.

CPM is only a first approximation of effectiveness. What matters most to marketers is not the simple cost of reaching a thousand people, but the cost of reaching a thousand people who are also potential customers and who also notice the marketers' message.

COUNTERTRADE

A form of international trading that gets around the difficulty of one party being short of tradable currency. Particularly popular between eastern and western Europe, where the former is frequently short of hard cash.

Countertrade can take several forms.

- **Barter.** For example, when the former Soviet Union paid for Pepsi Cola with vodka.
- **Compensation deals.** Payment is partly in goods and partly in an acceptable currency.
- **Counter-purchase.** Payment is in currency, but only on the understanding that the currency will be used to purchase the buying country's goods.
- **Buy-back deals.** A country exporting (say) a chemical plant or machinery for making television tubes accepts partial payment in the form of output from the factory that it is equipping.

COUNTLINE

The small items of confectionery that are placed near the till in supermarkets and newsagents. Countlines are designed to attract customers into making last-minute impulse purchases as they wait in line to pay for other goods.

COUPON

A certificate which gives the consumer a price reduction on a specific PRODUCT. Coupons can be included in print ADVERTISING mailed to householders, or they can be enclosed in or printed on a product's PACKAGING.

In the USA coupons are heavily used by consumer-goods manufacturers, despite the fact that their redemption rate is usually less than 5%. Big city newspapers often have large shopping sections stuffed with coupon offers.

Coupons are commonly used to encourage the purchase of a new product. When used to stimulate sales of a mature product they represent a form of price reduction that is more subtle than straightforward price cutting, and less likely to be noticed by competitors.

Low redemption rates can become a problem for manufacturers who use coupons. Retailers are sometimes tempted to redeem the coupons from the manufacturers, but give the price reduction on products other than the couponed ones. In other words, retailers allow the discounted amount to be set off against the customer's total bill, thus destroying the point of the PROMOTION.

COVERAGE

The percentage of a TARGET MARKET that has at least one opportunity to see an advertisement during a particular campaign.

Ads are the cave art of the 20th century.
Marshall McLuhan

CPM

See COST PER MILLE.

CREATIVE

The department in an ADVERTISING AGENCY that is involved in coming up with the ideas for advertisements and the artistic fulfilment of them, primarily composed of copywriters and graphic artists.

Behind the expression lies the idea that even in the irreverent world of ADVERTISING there are two cultures: art and science; producers and sellers; creators and managers. In this scheme of things most activity in advertising agencies (as elsewhere) arises from a time-consuming but creative resolution of the tension between these opposite poles.

> *First, make yourself a reputation for being a creative genius. Second, surround yourself with partners who are better than you. Third, leave them to get on with it.*
> David Ogilvy

CROSS-SELLING

Placing complementary products close to each other in a store in the hope that the customer who is tempted to buy one will spot the other and fall for that as well. For example, place women's skirts close to their blouses and jumpers; or bacon close to eggs.

CUSTOM BUILT

Something that is made according to a customer's particular specifications.

CUSTOMER

A person who buys goods or services. For some time now the customer has, as the old saying would have it, truly been king. Companies bend over backwards to improve their customer service; "customer focus" is the new object of their strategy; and their prices are honed to the bone in order to give the customer the best deal possible.

A customer is not necessarily the same thing as a consumer. Mothers are customers of baby-food manufacturers; but babies are the consumers of the manufacturers' products.

Companies that confuse customers with consumers can make big mistakes. Coca-Cola, for instance, used to pitch its advertising consistently at sporty macho males. But although they were the consumers of cola, they were not the customers. The customer was their wife or mother, and she was more impressed by price cuts on supermarkets' OWN-LABEL colas than by Coca-Cola's ability to make her son reach higher on a basketball court. So when a number of own-label colas hit the shelves in the early 1990s, they gained a remarkably high market share in a very short space of time (much of it at Coca-Cola's expense).

CUSTOMER PROFILE
A description of a business's customers in terms of their age, income, education, job, social habits, and so on.

Newspapers and magazines frequently produce profiles of their readers in order to tell advertisers what sort of person they are reaching by putting an advertisement in the publication. It is quite surprising how many of these readers are said to buy second homes, fast cars, and first-class airline tickets.

CUSTOMER PROPOSITION
The general idea that a product aims to convey to a potential customer. For example, Seven-Up's proposition to its customers is "Drink me and you'll feel fresh and clean". Pedigree Chum dog food says to its customers: "Buy me and you'll have a bouncy, energetic dog". If you want a lazy, sluggish dog, then Pedigree Chum's proposition is not for you.

CUSTOMER SERVICE
Once upon a time it was thought that goods were goods and services were services and never the twain would meet. Nowadays most people realise that there are few services that do not involve some goods – think of all the paper that comes with running a bank account, for example – and even fewer goods that do not involve some sort of

service. This service can take a variety of forms.

- AFTER-SALES SERVICE, such as repairs and replacement and/or a GUARANTEE.
- The provision of credit.
- Technical advice.
- Ease of contact (for example, through free-phone numbers).
- Complaints services.
- Maintenance.
- Information services.

In general, the more technologically complicated a PRODUCT, the more important is the service component. In the sale of INDUSTRIAL GOODS, and of consumer products such as cars or computers, the service component may be at least as important as the product itself in clinching a sale. Pundits agree that an important key to competitive advantage today lies in service, and the QUALITY of it.

CUSTOMISATION

The refining of traditionally mass-produced products to suit individual consumers. The use of information technology in production processes has enabled customisation to extend a long way. For example, in a number of stores in the United States Levi jeans can be tailor-made. A customer's measurements are fed into a computer and passed to the central manufacturing unit where they are read into machines which then cut and sew a customised garment.

DAGMAR
See DEFINING ADVERTISING GOALS FOR MEASURED ADVERTISING RESULTS.

DAR
See DAY-AFTER-RECALL.

DATA MINING
The technically complex extraction and manipulation of electronic data in order to enhance the marketing process. For example, computers might be programmed to "mine" their database of customers so as to come up with the names and addresses of everybody who has a birthday on that day. Those people can then be sent a goodwill card, for example, or a proposal for more life assurance.

DATA PROTECTION
The legal limitations imposed on the use of information about individuals, especially in electronic form. Thus in many countries individuals have a formal right to be told (when they ask) what information a company or credit-rating organisation holds about them.

DATA WAREHOUSING
The storing (ie, warehousing) of electronic data in an organisation's computer system in such a way that it is easy to search the data and extract from it information that may in future be useful to the people in the organisation – for marketing or other purposes.

DATABASE
An organised set of files which provide a common pool of information for several users. Databases about a company's customers are increasingly being held on computer and run by MARKETING departments. They can include information about both existing and potential customers and their characteristics, their buying methods, and their uses of products and services.

Databases can also include information about

competitors and other external variables that have to be taken into account when planning strategies.

In an age when information is a key part of a company's ability to provide QUALITY competitive products and services for a targeted market of customers who can benefit from those products and services, the construction and use of relevant databases is critical to success.

DATABASE MARKETING

The intelligent use of DATABASES for marketing purposes. (See also DATA MINING.)

If the 1960s was the decade of mass marketing, the 1970s of segmentation and line extensions, and the 1980s of micro-marketing, the 1990s will be the decade of one-to-one marketing.
Tom Peters

DATE STAMPING

The marking of perishable food products with a date by which the product should be sold and (in many cases) a date by which it should be consumed. Date stamping is a legal requirement in many countries.

DAY-AFTER-RECALL

Day-after-recall (DAR) is a method of analysing the impact of an advertisement (particularly of one appearing on television) by finding out what percentage of people can remember it on the day after it has appeared.

DEALER BRAND

A BRAND name put on a product by a middleman, usually a RETAILER; for example, Ann Page at the A&P stores in the USA, or St Michael at the UK's Marks and Spencer. Sometimes known as "own label" or "DISTRIBUTOR brand".

The increasing success of these brands reflects the growing power of big retail chains. In certain foodstuffs (tinned vegetables and cereals, for example) the market share of dealer brands has increased dramatically in recent years, reflecting their lower price and the fact that many consumers put more value on the dealer brand name than they do on the brand name of the traditional manufacturer.

DECISION CLUSTER
The bringing together by consumers of a number of buying decisions. If they buy a chicken they also buy stuffing; if they buy a pen they also buy ink, and so on.

DECISION-MAKING UNIT
In industrial buying, decisions about which suppliers' goods or services to purchase are not made as they are by a single consumer acting alone. Purchasing decisions are reached by a process of consultation between a number of people.

This group of people is referred to as a decision-making unit (DMU) and needs to be carefully identified by industrial sales people.

Several specific roles have been identified in the typical DMU. Since marketers love acronyms, these too have been turned into one: BUILD.

- **Buyer:** executes the purchase and is concerned mostly with price.
- **User:** uses the product, and is concerned first with performance.
- **Influencer:** the technical expert who provides guidelines for the decision.
- **Lodgekeeper:** controls information flows and access to others.
- **Decider:** formally authorises the purchase and is concerned with internal policy aspects of the decision.

Within the computer industry different companies have focused their MARKETING on different groups. IBM, for example, has gone for the Ds, the deciders. These are people who are not computer literate, but who know that they cannot be criticised for opting for such an impressive market leader as IBM. Digital, on the other hand, has gone for the Is, the technical experts.

DE-DUPLICATION

The process of combining two lists of names and addresses so that those common to both lists are not duplicated. Sending the same piece of DIRECT MAIL twice to the same address at the same time is wasteful and may be counterproductive in that it turns the recipient against the message that it carries. (See LIST BROKER.)

DEFINING ADVERTISING GOALS FOR MEASURED ADVERTISING RESULTS

The title of an influential essay written by Russell Colley in 1961, commonly known by the acronym DAGMAR. The essay provided a framework for thinking about an elusive goal: how to measure the effect that ADVERTISING has (and thus to find out which advertising expenditure is worthwhile).

To some extent the only measure of advertising's success is increased sales, but that is a long-term achievement. In the short term it is possible to measure changes in awareness and ATTITUDE. These provide clues about the effectiveness of advertising as consumers move through various preliminary stages of foreplay on their way to consummating a purchase. (See also AIDA and the HIERARCHY OF EFFECTS.)

DEMARKETING

The process of discouraging consumers from buying or consuming. Governments demarket cigarettes by requiring that health warnings be printed on every pack. "Share your bath with someone tonight" was a creative slogan once used by a UK water authority to demarket water during a summer drought.

Raising prices or restricting DISTRIBUTION as a form of rationing can also be regarded as demarketing.

DEMOGRAPHICS

Facts about the composition of a population (its age, sex, family size, family income, occupation, education, religion, race, nationality, and so on). Demographic analysis reveals important MARKET-

ING information that affects consumer demand – for example, changes in class structure, family composition and age profile.

The baby boom provided marketing opportunities for food manufacturers like Heinz and Gerber ("Babies are our only business") and Johnson & Johnson (makers of baby powder). As the birth rate fell and the number of elderly people increased, new opportunities were perceived: Gerber switched to insurance ("Gerber now babies the over-50s"); Johnson & Johnson repositioned its baby powder and shampoo as products for adults as well as children.

The increase in the number of working mothers, the growth of the Hispanic population in the USA, and the polarisation of populations into the "haves" and the urban underclass (the "have-nots"), are other demographic factors with important marketing implications.

At least as significant are shifting distributions of wealth. In many western nations the first generation of post-war business creators (and home owners) is dying off and/or passing on its wealth to the next generation, most of whom are in the 45–59 age group. What will they do with this windfall since most will by then have built businesses and bought houses of their own? It presents great marketing opportunities.

DEPARTMENT STORE

Stores that are traditionally located in the heart of central shopping areas in large cities, carrying a wide range of product classes, typically clothing, home furnishings and household goods. Department stores also give much attention to display and service. The first department store in the world is said to have been Bon Marché, which opened in Paris in 1852.

To support the high rents in these central locations, and their heavy staffing, department stores have operated on a high mark-up basis. In recent years many have had to close, reflecting intense competition from both discounters and self-service stores selling similar product categories.

They have also been affected by the decline of the central city shopping area. As a result, many have opened satellite stores in suburban shopping centres. As local authorities realise how this has had the effect of hollowing out urban centres, they have been devising schemes to persuade department stores and shopping malls to come back.

DEPTH INTERVIEW

An unstructured interview used for MARKET-RESEARCH purposes. Respondents talk freely under prompting and guidance from a researcher, usually a psychologist, who tries to uncover deep or hidden levels of motivation and behaviour. Psychological techniques, such as word association and sentence or story completion, may be used.

Depth interviews require highly skilled interviewers, and that makes them very costly. Nevertheless they are a significant tool in MOTIVATIONAL RESEARCH.

DERIVED DEMAND

A MARKETING concept derived from economics. Industrial marketers do not sell directly to consumers but to intermediary manufacturers. The demand for INDUSTRIAL GOODS and services is thus "derived" from the demand for the consumer goods which require the intermediary product. Thus the demand for the machinery to make tin cans is derived from the demand for products which are packaged in cans.

DESIGN

There are more than 25 different dictionary definitions of the word "design". In general, industrial design is the process of determining the appearance of things that are used by industry. It is often divided into three different categories.

1 PRODUCT design. The look of the products themselves.
2 Environmental design. The appearance of offices and factories.

3 Systems design. The design of computer networks, office information systems, and so on.

Something like a calendar will have elements of all three categories: it is a product, and will be designed as such; but it is also a piece of office furnishing; and it is a sort of information system. It will have design elements to take account of all of these facets.

> *Design is the conscious effort to impose meaningful order.*
> Victor Papanek

DESIGNER LABEL
The much valued label attached to a piece of clothing that proves it comes from a highly-rated designer. Once upon a time labels were always hidden discreetly inside the clothing. Today they are often attached to the outside where they are a clearly visible badge of good taste.

DESK RESEARCH
Research using secondary data that can be found by somebody sitting at a desk. This is usually the first stage in any MARKET RESEARCH project. Find out what is already known about a MARKET before setting out to do FIELD RESEARCH in order to collect primary data. The INTERNET has dramatically increased the scope of desk research in recent years.

DIARY PANEL
A diary panel consists of a number of consumers who use diaries to keep a regular (daily, weekly, and so on) record of all their purchases of a number of selected products. The Market Research Corporation of America (MCA) uses 7,500 families located throughout the USA. They note all their food and drug purchases during the week, and the analysis of their diaries is offered for sale. Other research companies collect diaries of, for example, people's television viewing habits.

D

DIFFERENTIATED MARKETING

See MARKET SEGMENTATION.

DIFFUSION

The process whereby a new PRODUCT is taken up by more and more consumers. At first, only individuals who are wholly confident about it, or who love taking risks, will buy it. Once these INNOVATORS have taken to the product, it will be tried by a larger group, known as EARLY ADOPTERS. They are the opinion-leaders who will influence wider acceptance of the product.

Diffusion can be speeded up by making ADOPTION seem less risky. Cosmetics manufacturers give samples away free or at a special introductory price; manufacturers install machines on a six-month trial basis; or (as in IBM's case) give away thousands of personal computers to US business schools in order quickly to secure consumer acceptance beyond the circle of early adopters.

DIRECT MAIL

The sending of ADVERTISING and promotional material directly to consumers. Usually associated with MAIL-ORDER selling, direct mail has a much wider range of purposes, including appeals for money and for political support. It is used by a large number of organisations, from American Express to *Time* magazine to specialist retailers like Banana Republic.

The great advantage of direct mail is that marketers can target their audience with great precision through the use of databases with many thousands, even millions, of names and addresses, each identified by demographic and consumption information. Such databases, which are often owned by specialist firms, make it possible for marketers to select carefully the most likely buyers of virtually any PRODUCT.

Although direct mail is sometimes disparagingly referred to as "junk mail", research suggests that fewer than one mailing in five goes into a waste bin unread.

DIRECT MARKETING

The shortest channel of DISTRIBUTION, when a manufacturer of a PRODUCT deals directly with the consumer. Farmers who advertise "Potatoes for Sale" at their gate, or "Pick your own Strawberries" are engaging in direct marketing. So are sales people who call directly at people's homes, be they selling insurance, cosmetics or encyclopedias.

MAIL ORDER accounts for the largest segment of direct marketing. Other forms are:

• telephone selling (see CALL CENTRE), a fast-growing method of direct marketing, particularly of financial services such as insurance;
• selling through newspaper or magazine advertisements;
• DIRECT MAIL, driven increasingly from a computerised DATABASE.

DIRECT RESPONSE ADVERTISING

The sort of advertisement which has a telephone number that customers can call immediately to order the goods or services being advertised. Long popular in the printed MEDIA, direct response advertising is being used increasingly in television advertisements, especially in the United States. There, charities often give a number for viewers to call as soon as the advertisement is off the air.

DIRECTIONAL POLICY MATRIX

A classification of products developed by the Shell oil company. It is based on two dimensions:

• the profitability of the MARKET segment in which the business operates;
• the competitive position of the business in that segment.

A PRODUCT's position on the matrix suggests its future; for example, the matrix's prognosis for a product with an average competitive position in a market that has a poor prospect of future profitability is of phased withdrawal from that market.

D

DISAFFECTED SURVIVOR
A category of consumer found widely across Europe (see LIFESTYLE).

DISCRETIONARY INCOME
That part of a consumer's DISPOSABLE INCOME that is not spoken for in advance in the form of mortgage or CONSUMER-CREDIT repayments, school fees, or other standing orders and direct debits.

Marketers are eternally looking for people with high levels of discretionary income. This is not the same as wealthy people; wealthy people may have high incomes that are almost all spoken for, particularly at certain stages in their lives.

Although EMPTY NESTERS, for example, expect their incomes to fall as they get older and retire, their discretionary income may actually rise as the expense of raising children in a large property gradually disappears.

DISPLAY ADVERTISING
The sort of peacock ADVERTISING that takes up a whole page of a magazine and shows off impressive artwork, graphics, photos and words, all of it eye-catchingly arranged.

DISPOSABLE INCOME
A slightly different economic concept from DISCRETIONARY INCOME. Disposable income is that income left to consumers after they have paid all compulsory levies from the state, such as direct income taxes, property taxes or wealth taxes. Disposable income will always be greater than discretionary income.

DISTRIBUTION
A key MARKETING function: the process of getting products to consumers. Although some manufacturers can and do sell direct to consumers (see DIRECT MARKETING), practical considerations require most to use a distribution system composed of independent middlemen, usually wholesalers and retailers.

These intermediaries carry out critically important marketing activities, such as buying and selling, sorting and storing, transporting and financing products as they move from producer to consumer. All of these activities are necessary functions if products are to be found by consumers in the right place at the right time and at the right price.

Distribution can also refer to a measure of market PENETRATION: the number of retail outlets which stock and sell a particular product as a percentage of all outlets that could possibly sell that product.

DISTRIBUTION CHANNEL

The network of organisations that moves goods from the manufacturer to the consumer. Increasingly, these networks incorporate electronic links of one sort or another – sophisticated software programmes for managing stock control, for example, or the telephone for DIRECT MARKETING and/or selling.

DISTRIBUTOR

A WHOLESALER of industrial products. Distributors are the major force in industrial distribution channels. Surprisingly, even in the USA most of them have continued to survive as relatively small business units.

Distributors sell goods to manufacturers. They also provide warehousing, and a range of other services such as delivery, credit, order processing and technical advice.

As sellers to manufacturers they need to be able to respond quickly to their customers' needs, so that production processes are not disrupted. As part of their ability to respond quickly, many distributors provide a repair service for the goods that they sell, acting as an agent on behalf of the original manufacturer.

DMU
See DECISION-MAKING UNIT.

DOWNMARKET
See UPMARKET.

DRIP CAMPAIGN

An ADVERTISING CAMPAIGN in which the advertisements are shown infrequently over a long period of time. The opposite of a drip campaign is a "burst".

DUMPING

Offering goods for sale in a foreign MARKET at prices lower than those prevailing in their domestic market. Dumping amounts to *prima facie* evidence of unfair competition and is against the rules of the World Trade Organisation, the successor to the General Agreement on Tariffs and Trade (GATT). Proof that dumping has taken place is, however, often difficult to establish. Exchange-rate fluctuations, and the use of transfer-PRICING methods that might themselves be quite legitimate, can blur the most genuine attempt to compare export prices with domestic prices.

The name of Durex, the condom manufactured by LRC, formerly the London Rubber Company, came "out of the air" according to its inventor, A.R. Reid, a former chairman of the company. It came to him while he was travelling on the train home from London to Southend-on-Sea. Apparently the names of other LRC contraceptives, Fetherlite and Gossamer, came to him in a similar way.

EARLY ADOPTERS

Those people who are quick to buy and to try new products and services. They are not the people who like to buy any new gadget that appears on the market. But they are more adventurous than most consumers, and their interest (or disinterest) tends to determine whether a new product is a success or not. (See also DIFFUSION.)

E-COMMERCE

Short for electronic commerce – commerce conducted on the INTERNET. Many companies are predicting phenomenal growth for e-commerce in the coming years, and the globe is pock-marked with experiments in marketing, selling, and paying for goods and services on the Net.

Initial problems focused on the difficulty in making financial details secure on a public network. Nobody is going to key in details of their credit card if they feel that every hacker from Rochester to Riga can then find it out and use it.

EFFIE AWARDS

The annual awards presented by the New York chapter of the American Marketing Association to ADVERTISING agencies and their clients for the QUALITY and effectiveness of advertisements in a number of different categories. Most nations have an equivalent form of annual advertising award. In Hong Kong they are called "Golden Junks"; in Turkey they are "Glass Apples".

ELASTICITY

An economic concept that relates the change in one variable to the change in another. A piece of elastic's elasticity is the extra distance it stretches for every extra unit of weight that is suspended from it. The elasticity of demand in a particular market is the change in sales that results from a unit increase or decrease in the PRODUCT's price.

ELECTRONIC POINT OF SALE

Commonly known by the acronym EPOS. A checkout counter that is equipped with the necessary electronic gadgetry to read a BAR CODE. The codes are passed over an electronic scanner placed in the counter, or are read by using a hand-held electronic light pen.

The information then passes into the store's computer where it can be used to maintain up-to-the-minute STOCK CONTROL. The information can also be printed out as a fully itemised receipt for the customer.

EPOS is not to be confused with EFTPOS (electronic funds transfer at the point of sale). EFTPOS refers to the electronic technology that enables consumers to pay for goods with a plastic card which debits their bank account directly and immediately. EFTPOS eliminates the time-consuming task of writing cheques, but it gives the customer no period of credit at all.

EMPTY NESTERS

Families whose children have flown the nest and set up their own independent households. Such people form an interesting group of consumers for marketers. They have particularly high levels of DISCRETIONARY INCOME because their housing costs have been reduced (by paying off the mortgage or moving to a smaller home) and the cost of supporting their children has also dropped dramatically.

Empty nesters (particularly those in the 50–60 age group) are increasingly having their discretionary income further enhanced by inheritance from parents who are dying later, and who are leaving ever larger capital sums.

EMULATOR

One of the categories in a well-known US classification of consumers (see LIFESTYLE).

END-USER

The consumer who actually uses a PRODUCT. This may not be the same as the person who is responsible for making the decision to purchase that product, which is an important point for marketers to remember. For example, babies do not decide what baby food they are to be the end-user of; and many men do not decide what suits, socks or shirts they are to be the end-users of.

ENVIRONMENTAL SCANNING
The systematic examination of the business environment with a view to identifying MARKETING opportunities and threats. The business environment includes competitors, the domestic economy, trade patterns, cultural and social trends, and technology. Nowadays it also includes attitudes to the environment itself. The powerful Green consumer movement has provided many marketing threats; but it has thrown up many marketing opportunities as well.

EPOS
See ELECTRONIC POINT OF SALE.

It takes up to 40 dumb animals to make a fur coat, but only one to wear it.
Anti-fur campaign

ETHICAL GOODS
An ADVERTISING industry expression for drugs and equipment that are sold to the medical profession and not directly to the general public. There are some peculiar MARKETING features associated with such products.

• They are sold to a relatively small group of knowledgeable consumers, each of which can be responsible (through their prescriptions) for a large amount of consumption.
• They are often produced by drug companies under patent, so they have no direct competition.

EXCLUSIVE DISTRIBUTION
The right given by a manufacturer to a RETAILER to be the sole vendor of the manufacturer's products in a given geographical area (a territory), similar in many ways to certain sorts of franchising. Business computers, high-quality luggage and fine

china are some of the products typically sold on an exclusive distribution basis.

The system gives manufacturers greater control over their DISTRIBUTION networks, especially with regard to their products' retail prices and the services that are offered with them.

EXHIBITION

Using large exhibition halls (often of over 100,000 square metres) for manufacturers in the same industry to test out their new products and to meet customers is a well-established practice in countries like Germany where some of the world's largest industrial exhibitions are held. The commonest reason cited for attending exhibitions is the "need to keep abreast of technology". In Germany they are also frequently an excuse for a "family outing".

Exhibitions can account for up to 20% of German companies' PROMOTION budgets. In the UK they are unlikely to account for more than 10%, even though research has shown that marketers there believe them to be the second best way (after the trade press) to launch a new product.

The exhibitions industry has become so big that it now has an exhibition of its own – called International Confex.

Experts should be always on tap, but never on top.
Anon

EXPECTATIONS

A word that economists have adopted to refer to people's beliefs about the economic future. To some extent these are self-fulfilling. If business people expect the future to be rosy they will invest more; the future is then indeed more likely to be rosy.

Expectations also play a great part in the business of MARKETING. To advertise a new PRODUCT as being something that it is not is more damaging than not to advertise it at all. If consumers' expectations are frustrated after they have purchased a product, not only will they not buy it again but they will also feel badly done by. They may then spread unfavourable WORD-OF-MOUTH ADVERTISING.

EXTENDED GUARANTEE

A GUARANTEE that a manufacturer offers (at a price) to a customer for a specified period of time beyond the term of the original guarantee. It is a prolonged insurance policy against breakdown. Some companies, as a marketing strategy, set the prices of the goods they sell low and then rely on extended guarantees for a large part of their profits. Logically, of course, a company that feels the need to offer extended guarantees cannot have a lot of confidence in the reliability of the products it is selling.

The name Exxon was the result of a search for a word that was meaningless and without connotation in any language. 10,000 names were produced by a computer. These were reduced to 234 by extensive opinion polls among 7,000 people; and thence to six. These six were then carefully examined for meaninglessness in more than 100 languages.

FACT BOOK

A file of information about a PRODUCT's history. Typically a fact book contains:

- data on the product's sales, DISTRIBUTION, and competition;
- a profile of its customers;
- any relevant MARKET-RESEARCH findings;
- a detailed record of the product's performance over time in relation to the MARKETING effort made on its behalf.

Fact books are retained by company BRAND managers and by ADVERTISING AGENCY account managers.

FAD

A PRODUCT that is suddenly and briefly taken up with great enthusiasm. It is characterised by rapid sales growth and almost equally rapid sales decline. Well-known fads include the Rubik cube, the Pet Rock and the skateboard.

FAMILY LIFE CYCLE

A description of the six ages of family man based on demographic data. The cycle has proved useful in defining the demand for certain goods and services because each age produces distinguishable needs and interests. The six stages of the cycle are as follows.

1 Young single people.
2 Young couples with no children.
3 Young couples with their youngest child under six.
4 Couples with dependent children.
5 Older couples with no children at home.
6 Older single people.

FASHION GOODS

Goods where style and DESIGN are all-important. Best illustrated by women's clothing, where what starts off in the haute couture salons of Paris and Milan is imitated by mass manufacturers. It then appears briefly in high-street shops before disappearing to make way for the next fashion goods that have been copied from the cat-walk. MARKETING goods with such a short shelf-life requires special skills.

FAST FOOD
The production of limited and standardised menus at self-service counters offering customers food to eat on the premises or to take away. Fast-food outlets have four particular characteristics.

1 The premises are bright, basic and clean.
2 The staff are trained to be cheerful and helpful.
3 The quality of the food is consistent.
4 The outlets are franchised.

Fast food has been one of the fastest-growing retailing INNOVATIONS in recent decades. Although hamburger joints, pizza parlours and fish 'n chip shops existed before 1952, there was no really fast food until the McDonald company raised its golden arches for the first time that year. McDonald's pioneering formula for hamburgers has been followed by formulae for pizza, chicken pieces, tacoes, doughnuts, croissants, and even fish 'n chips.

FAST-MOVING CONSUMER GOODS
The kind of products that are usually sold in supermarkets and which move off the shelves quickly, like toothpaste and chewing gum. Fast-moving consumer goods (FMCGS) require in-store stocks of them to be constantly replenished. Hence at any one moment there are more FMCGS on the road than anywhere else.

Fiat was founded in 1899 as Fabbrica Italiana Automobili Torino, the Italian automobile company of Turin.

FIELD RESEARCH
MARKET RESEARCH carried out in the "field", through

interviews, GROUP DISCUSSION, and so on, as opposed to DESK RESEARCH. In practice, field research is more likely to be carried out in the street than anywhere else.

FLAGSHIP
The pre-eminent store or product in a company's portfolio of products or stores. Thus Bird's Eye's flagship brand could be said to be fish fingers, because although the company sells everything from custard to frozen peas, fish fingers are the brand for which the company is best known.

Likewise Marks & Spencer's flagship store is the one near London's Marble Arch. Not only does it have the highest sales per square foot of any of the group's stores, but it is also the outlet where Marks & Spencer experiments with new products or ranges.

FLANKER BRAND
A new BRAND that is introduced by a company which already markets a brand in the same PROD-UCT category. For example, a new chocolate bar from Mars or a diet mayonnaise by Hellmann's. (See also LINE EXTENSION.)

FLASH PACK
A package on which a sales PROMOTION message (usually a price reduction) is printed prominently. Products in flash packs are offered in limited quantities and/or for limited periods of time.

FMCGS
See FAST-MOVING CONSUMER GOODS.

FOCUS GROUP
A group of people gathered together for an informal discussion for the purposes of MARKET RESEARCH. The interviewer/chairperson has an agenda of topics to cover, but questionnaires are not used.

Interaction within the group is designed to encourage wide-ranging exploration of a subject. Focus groups are typically used for NEW PRODUCT

DEVELOPMENT in order to test both ideas and products. They are also used for QUALITATIVE RESEARCH on existing products, and sometimes by ADVERTISING agencies to try out new bits of copy.

Almost everybody knows that Ford is the name of Henry Ford, the man who founded the company. But Chevrolet, Chrysler, Citröen and Porsche are also the names of men who were closely involved with the development of the cars named after them.

FRANCHISE

A contractual agreement in which one party (the franchiser) sells the right to market goods or services to another party (the franchisee). McDonald's and Kentucky Fried Chicken are long-standing examples of successful retail franchises that started in the USA. There are other examples that started in Europe (and outside the fast-food business) like Benetton and Body Shop.

Franchising can also take place at the wholesale level. Both Coca-Cola and Pepsi Cola built up their worldwide businesses by franchising their secret ingredients to wholesale bottlers who then produced and bottled the beverages, and distributed them to retailers. Hence the common observation that the two mighty colas taste slightly different in different countries.

In retail franchising the franchiser provides the franchisee with a large number of MARKETING services. In return, the franchisee purchases equipment and supplies, pays franchising fees (often a large initial fee) and, frequently, a percentage of revenues.

The franchisee is usually given exclusive selling rights in a particular area, although not by Benetton. It has successfully defended its right to grant a franchise to shops on opposite sides of the same street.

FREQUENCY DISTRIBUTION

A common way of presenting MARKET-RESEARCH

statistics, according to the frequency with which particular responses are given. For example, suppose a researcher is asking people for their response to an advertisement that they have just seen. They may be offered several choices of response: very warm, warm, indifferent, hostile, or very hostile.

The researcher's findings can then be plotted as a chart, with the number of respondents on one axis and the type of response on the other. Such a chart, showing the frequency distribution, will give a clearer picture of the overall response to the advertisement.

FULFILMENT

The process of fulfilling orders received through DIRECT-MAIL selling. In the case of a magazine subscription, for example, fulfilment will involve:

● sending magazines to the subscriber for the period of time paid for;
● sending reminders as and when the subscription needs to be renewed;
● leaving a trail so that any problems with a particular subscriber can be followed up.

Most fulfilment systems nowadays are computer-based. (See KEY CODE.)

FULFILMENT HOUSE

A firm that carries out the FULFILMENT of a direct mail campaign – ie, the gathering of all the orders for the advertiser's products or services and the DISTRIBUTION of those products.

FUNCTIONALISM

An approach to the study of MARKETING that focuses on the functions of marketing rather than its institutions. Functionalism is particularly associated with Ed McGarry who defined the functions of marketing as being the following.

● **Contactual:** searching out buyers and sellers.
● **Merchandising:** fitting the goods to MARKET

requirements.

- **PRICING:** selecting a price high enough to make production possible and low enough to induce users to accept the goods.
- **Propaganda:** conditioning buyers or sellers to a favourable attitude towards the PRODUCT or its sponsor.
- **Physical DISTRIBUTION:** transporting and storing the goods.
- **Termination:** consummation of the marketing process.

GAP ANALYSIS

A procedure for discovering MARKETING opportunities represented by gaps in a MARKET. There are three important areas in which to look for gaps:

- a neglected consumer group;
- a deficiency in existing product offerings;
- an area suitable for exploitation because of some new technological development.

Market researchers have developed sophisticated techniques for conducting gap analysis (see PERCEPTUAL MAPPING).

GENERATION X

The title of a book by Douglas Coupland that defined the generation in America born between the years 1960 and 1980. The book tells the tale of three young people disillusioned with the corporate rat-race that they see as being at the heart of modern life. Generation Xers do not look for long-term careers, they prefer a series of short-term contractual arrangements.

GENERIC NAME

The name of a class or category of products; for example, "computers" or "soups". Sometimes the name of a successful BRAND comes to be used as a generic name: Kleenex means paper handkerchiefs in general; and Hoover means vacuum cleaner.

GENERICS

Goods that are sold with little or no ADVERTISING or PROMOTION, and usually in simple PACKAGING. Often referred to as Brand X goods, generics represent a response to criticism that too much money is spent on MARKETING, and that "no frills" products allow substantial price reductions. Generics have made strong inroads into commodity-type household products like soap and toilet paper.

In general, generics are goods that are non-proprietary, in particular drugs and pharmaceuticals that have come "off patent", like Anadin and

Paracetamol. Generic drugs can be manufactured and sold by anybody.

GET-A-LIFERS

The British equivalent of GENERATION X, the twenty-somethings who reacted against the Thatcherite "Till death us do part" approach to work. A favourite word of the get-a-lifers is 'holistic'. They want work in moderation, they want friends-a-plenty, and they don't want divorce. The identification of these attitudes has obvious implications for future consumption and for employment.

GLOBAL PRODUCT

A PRODUCT that has a BRAND name which is universally recognised; for example, Coca-Cola, McDonald's, IBM, Levi and Hilton. Some marketers speculate that the world will shortly be dominated by global products because of the production and MARKETING capability of large multinational companies. Some shoppers suspect that it already is.

The idea of global products gained respectability through a famous article in the *Harvard Business Review* of May/June 1983. Called "The globalisation of markets", it was written by Theodore Levitt, a professor of marketing at Harvard. The article started by asserting that:

A powerful force now drives the world towards a single converging commonality, and that force is technology … the result is a new commercial reality: the emergence of global markets for standardised consumer products on a previously unimagined scale of magnitude. Corporations geared to this new reality benefit from enormous economies of scale in production, distribution, marketing and management.

The marketing of global products makes assumptions about the universality of human needs and wants, but marketers recognise that global brands cannot be marketed in the same way in every country. Procter & Gamble markets its Pampers disposable nappies in over 70 countries, but in each country the MARKETING MIX is tailored to local requirements in terms of price, DISTRIBUTION and ADVERTISING.

Brand names sometimes encounter unexpected difficulties when crossing international borders. For example, Ireland's Irish Mist liqueur comes up against unexpected problems in selling to German-speaking markets; in German mist means manure. Likewise the UK's Cadbury Schweppes declined to buy a French soft drink that was offered to it. The drink was called Pschitt.

Timotei shampoo is one of the few completely new products over the last 20 years that has successfully gone global. It started life in Finland as a small deodorant brand within the Unilever empire. In Finnish its name means "grass". But the product wilted. Then Unilever's Swedish company spotted its potential as a pure and mild shampoo in an environmentally conscious age; and it has not looked back.

Goodyear and Firestone, which now sound such suitable names for tyre companies that we cannot imagine they were not specially created for the purpose, are in fact the names of the men who set up the companies.

GROUP DISCUSSION
Synonymous with FOCUS GROUP.

GUARANTEE
A promise given by a manufacturer to a consumer that a product is of a certain standard, and that if it is not, then the manufacturer will make good any shortcomings. Guarantees are important in the MARKETING of certain consumer durables. They can prove expensive if a manufacturer has to replace large numbers of faulty goods.

In the USA (where guarantees are usually called warranties) manufacturers must, by law, produce a clearly written statement about what they promise in their warranties. The warranty must be neither unfair nor deceptive, and it must be clear as to whether it is a full warranty, or limited in some way. For example, it is common to limit the guarantee on a car to the cost of parts for five years, and of labour for one year.

HABIT BUYING

When a consumer repeatedly buys the same BRAND. Habit buying is believed to imply the absence of dissatisfaction with a brand rather than any positive loyalty to it. It is usually associated with the purchase of a LOW-INVOLVEMENT PRODUCT and can often be broken by an attractive sales PROMOTION.

> *We're not in the hamburger business; we're in show business.*
> Ray Kroc, founder of McDonald's

HARD SELL

Anything that is deemed to be aggressive selling. That can vary greatly depending on the MARKET in which the selling is taking place. In a high-class boutique a hard sell can be as soft as a silk blouse. At a fruit stall in the street it may be as hard as a plum stone.

HARVESTING STRATEGY

The reaping of short-term profit from a PRODUCT prior to withdrawing it from the MARKET. If it has been decided that a product is coming to the end of its PRODUCT LIFE CYCLE, MARKETING expenditure on it will be reduced; typically, ADVERTISING will be withdrawn. Because the effects of earlier advertising will still be felt, the product will continue to sell, ideally producing attractive net profits during its last days.

Some products' last days can spread into years if large enough bands of die-hard customers exist. Ipana toothpaste and Lifebuoy soap both lived on profitably years after their marketing support had been withdrawn.

HEAVY USER

That segment of a market which accounts for the bulk of its sales. Not all markets have a pronounced concentration on a few buyers, but where such heavy users exist there is little point in directing MARKETING effort at other groups.

Heineken has said that it would use the medium of DIRECT MAIL to advertise its lager to the 9% of men who drink 65% of its output if only there were a way of finding out their names and addresses.

HIERARCHY OF EFFECTS

The steps in the process of persuading somebody to buy something. The hierarchy moves through the following stages:

- awareness;
- knowledge;
- liking;
- preference;
- conviction;
- purchase.

MARKETING communications are constructed with this hierarchy in mind; and sales people will often follow these steps in making a sales presentation. (See also AIDA.)

HIGH-INVOLVEMENT PRODUCT

A PRODUCT over which consumers take time and trouble to reach a purchasing decision; goods for which they shop around, comparing prices or financing arrangements.

Consumers take this sort of trouble over their purchases when there are elements of self-image, cost or product performance involved. Cars, homes, fitted kitchens, hi-fi systems and package-tour holidays are examples of high-involvement products.

HIGH STREET

A general term used to refer to the typical shopping street in the centre of an ordinary town in the UK. In many cases such a street will actually be called High Street. (In the USA the equivalent is Main Street.)

Such streets are being displaced by out-of-town superstores and shopping malls. But the expression is still widely used to refer to retailing practices, as in "You won't find a dress like that on the high street" or "There's no sign of a recession yet on the high street".

HIRE PURCHASE

A form of CONSUMER CREDIT that involves an agreement that is both a hire and a purchase agreement. In effect, the consumer hires the PRODUCT and pays rent regularly (for the hire) for a pre-arranged length of time. With the last rental payment the hitherto hired goods become the property of the consumer.

HIT RATE

The inverse of the number of people that have to be approached before a salesman makes a sale. Thus if a salesman of household cleaning products makes one sale at every 50 houses that he visits, his hit rate is 0.02. (See COLD CALLING.)

HOARDING

See BILLBOARD.

HOME AUDIT

MARKET RESEARCH conducted in the home by using a DIARY PANEL to record on a regular basis (weekly or monthly) what products householders buy, and how often they buy them.

The Hoover was first manufactured and marketed by a company owned by William Henry Hoover. But the Hoover was actually invented by one J. Murray Spangler, a caretaker from Ohio. We could have been cleaning our carpets today with a Spangler.

HOME PAGE

The first (introductory) screen of information given by a particular company or organisation at its WEB SITE. As companies use their Web sites more and more for marketing purposes, it is increasingly important that the design of the home page is user-friendly. It should help to lead "browsers" gently through the rest of the information that the company wants them to see.

HOUSEHOLD

The people who live together in a single house, and who constitute the fundamental unit in much MARKET RESEARCH. Households are of particular interest because most consumption is done by household units rather than by individuals. The purchase of many consumer durables, like vacuum cleaners, dishwashers, or video-cassette recorders, is more closely related to the number of households in a population (each of which can contain five or six people), than it is to the number of individuals.

The average size of a household varies greatly throughout the world and even in regions as relatively homogeneous as Europe. In Denmark and Sweden the average household size is 2.15 people only; in Denmark one in every three households has only one person in it. In Ireland the average is 3.83 people and in the former Soviet Union 3.93.

Even countries like Italy and the UK, which have roughly the same population, the same GDP and the same living standard, differ considerably in the size of their households. In the UK the average size is 2.57 people; in Italy it is 3.01.

The Hovis loaf started life in 1887 as Smith's Patent Germ Bread. The name Hovis came out of a competition in which the winner invented a contraction of hominis vis, *the strength of man.*

HYPERMARKET

A French invention, the word being an anglicisation of *hypermarché*. The hypermarket is a store that is bigger than a SUPERMARKET. It also sells a wider range of products than the FAST-MOVING CONSUMER GOODS that consumers have come to expect to find in a supermarket.

Because of their size hypermarkets are always found on out-of-town sites surrounded by vast car parks. They can thus only be reached by affluent and physically capable consumers who have their own cars.

IMAGE

The picture, or feeling, or association which the name of a BRAND conjures up in a person's mind. A PRODUCT's image is what that product means to a person. For example, Volvo cars mean "safety"; Jaguar cars mean "class".

Nations also have images, and those images can change over time: "Made in Japan" used to mean cheap and shoddy; now it means high QUALITY, high-tech and high prices.

In recent years, advertisers of consumer products have paid less attention to communicating a product's ATTRIBUTES, and have concentrated more on creating a strong product image.

> *An ounce of image is worth a pound of performance.*
> Lawrence Peter

IMPULSE BUYING

Spur of the moment decisions to buy, made at the time of purchase. Goods which are apt to be bought impulsively (magazines, sweets, chewing gum) are usually placed close to the POINT OF SALE. Goods which are bought routinely, like cereals or shampoo, may also be subject to impulse buying.

> *If every new product is stamped "improved" then what were we buying before?*
> Anon

INCENTIVE MARKETING

An umbrella term for all the special techniques used to persuade consumers to buy products; for example, SAMPLING, PREMIUM OFFER, COUPON, SELF-LIQUIDATING OFFER. More commonly called sales PROMOTION.

INDUSTRIAL ADVERTISING

See BUSINESS-TO-BUSINESS ADVERTISING.

INDUSTRIAL GOODS

Goods that are purchased mainly for use in the production of other goods, in contrast to consumer goods. They include such things as machines, tools, components and lubricants. Few goods are exclusively industrial; for example, lubricants are also sold directly to consumers.

INERTIA SELLING

A form of selling familiar to anyone who has ever belonged to a book club. If you do not cancel the monthly selection then you receive the book. The sale is made as a result of inertia, that is, the customer's failure to take any action to stop it.

Few human beings are proof against the implied
flattery of rapt attention.
Jack Woodford

INNOVATION

The process of developing and introducing a new PRODUCT, or new product DESIGN, to a market. Under pressure of competition, companies try to preserve their competitive advantage by continuous product innovation. As the rate of innovation increases, the time that a product has in which to produce a profit for the company is reduced. That puts more pressure on the company to innovate, and so the spiral of innovation continues.

The successful management of the process of innovation is crucial to most companies' success. Some concentrate their efforts on bringing out products based on established market demand; a new detergent, for example, or a new line of cosmetics. Other companies are true innovators, developing technological firsts, like the home computer or the compact disc player.

The US company 3M insists that at least 25% of its sales come from products that are less than five years old. This is one way to check that the process of innovation is continuing at a satisfactory pace.

INNOVATORS

Consumers who are the first to try new products. Research suggests that innovators tend to be well-educated, well-informed, well-to-do, open-minded, upwardly mobile, and reachable by the mass MEDIA. They are also only a small percentage of the total population compared with other identified consumer types.

	%
Innovators	2.5
Early adopters	13.5
Early majority	34.0
Late majority	34.0
Laggards	16.0

The same people will not be innovators for every PRODUCT. A new method of seed drilling will appeal to one group of innovators, while digital audio tape will appeal to another. Marketers always try to identify the innovator group for any given product, and concentrate their initial efforts on them.

INSTALMENT CREDIT

An arrangement between a buyer and a seller whereby the buyer pays for goods or services in instalments over time; the vendor thus effectively extends credit to the buyer, even though there may be no formal payment of interest involved.

The rich are different. They'll never know the pleasure of paying the last instalment.
Anon

INSTITUTIONAL ADVERTISING

Most ADVERTISING is concerned with goods and services, but there are many organisations which simply advertise themselves. Companies whose brands are conspicuously linked with the company name, such as DuPont or Zanussi, anticipate that favourable public reaction to their corporate advertising will spill over to their products.

Companies whose operations may create public hostility, such as mining, oil, chemical or nuclear-power companies, use institutional advertising to try and counteract negative reactions. In the USA, for example, Chevron Oil advertised the fact that it was preserving the habitat of a tiny endangered species of butterfly in the middle of its giant refinery and right next to the huge Los Angeles international airport.

Giant multinational conglomerates whose portfolios include a wide range of businesses also use institutional advertising to establish their name. United Technologies ran a series of advertisements in US newspapers which featured homilies on profound but non controversial subjects. Only the name of the company appeared at the bottom of the page; there was no mention of any PRODUCT. The series proved very popular, eliciting thousands of requests for reprints.

INTEGRATED COMMUNICATIONS

A popular phrase with MARKETING directors that refers to the co-ordination of all aspects of product PROMOTION, from ADVERTISING to DIRECT MAIL. (See also ABOVE-THE-LINE and BELOW-THE-LINE.)

INTENTIONS

Attempts are sometimes made to forecast future sales on the basis of consumers' stated intentions to buy. Research is undertaken, particularly in the field of INDUSTRIAL GOODS, to ascertain such "intentions". However, since the respondent has little to lose by his or her answers, the results of such research have to be interpreted with caution.

INTERACTIVE MARKETING

An approach to MARKETING that stresses that both buyers and sellers are active in decision-making, particularly in industrial markets. Standard models of marketing have been criticised for being too deterministic, suggesting that suppliers have total control over the marketing process and that customers are passive.

Interactive marketing stresses that marketing

success is dependent on the competence and ability of the individuals and organisations involved in the process of interaction. It maintains that an understanding of the relationship and interdependence between supplier and customer is essential to good marketing. Important aspects of the interaction are:

- the atmosphere surrounding the relationship;
- the degree of co-operation and conflict;
- the overall social distance between buyers and sellers.

INTERNATIONAL MARKETING
Companies are increasingly selling their products outside their domestic MARKET. Some foreign brands have become so familiar that consumers assume they are manufactured by indigenous companies. For example, who knows that Nescafé is made by a Swiss company; Baskin and Robbins ice-cream by a British company; and Crest toothpaste by a US company?

INTERNET
Also known as the Net, a global network of computer systems with a universal means of access. The Internet has enormous, as yet largely untapped potential for marketing purposes.

INTRANET
A network of computer systems with limited access – via a password or other link – as opposed to the INTERNET which is open to all. Intranets are increasingly popular within companies where the rapid dissemination of knowledge among a large workforce may be of vital competitive importance.

INVESTOR RELATIONS
A sub-set of PUBLIC RELATIONS that became fashionable in the stockmarket-driven euphoria of the 1980s. Investor relations is concerned with improving communications between a company and its shareholders.

Traditionally companies come in two shapes:

- private companies that are family-owned and family-run;
- public companies that are owned by distant shareholders and run by a completely different group of people called managers.

Investor relations is concerned with the second type, and with helping managers to make their shareholders become more involved and concerned with the company that they "own".

JINGLE

A catchy tune which when it is played as part of a television commercial can be a powerful MARKETING tool.

Jingles used to be written and commissioned especially for particular advertisements, and a very small number of them would subsequently become popular hit songs. In recent years, however, advertisers have increasingly used snippets of popular old songs as jingles. For example, they have used songs which evoke nostalgia among BABY BOOMERS – today's big spenders – for the years of their youth. The trend was led by Levi Strauss, which has always (and very successfully) put nostalgia at the centre of its ADVERTISING message.

> *If you've got nothing to say, sing it.*
> Advertising industry advice

JUDGMENT SAMPLING

The selection of respondents for a market survey on the basis of criteria judged by the researcher to be the most appropriate for the purposes of the research.

Judgment sampling is most frequently used in industrial MARKET RESEARCH. In an industry dominated by a few manufacturers, the researcher may decide that a sample which is representative of those few is more significant than one which attempts to embrace all manufacturers in the industry.

JUNK MAIL

Promotional and ADVERTISING material of all kinds that arrives, unsolicited, in the daily mail. The judgment that the term implies is picturesque, but not entirely accurate. (See DIRECT MAIL.)

KEY CODE

The six-digit alphanumeric code that marketers put on their direct mailshots (usually near to the address) so that they can analyse the response to DIRECT MAIL. Key coding enables them to find out things like:

- which (purchased) list a respondent came from;
- what type of offer was made to him or her;
- what social category he or she belongs to.

Kleenex is a word that was invented in the 1920s, one of a spate of contemporary no-meaning names that ended in "x". The spate included Lux, Pyrex and Cutex.

KNOCKING COPY

Copy that is critical of a competitor's PRODUCT. (See COMPARATIVE ADVERTISING.)

Kodak, generally agreed to be one of the most successful brand names ever (having two essential ingredients: alliteration and the "k" sound), was chosen by George Eastman in 1888. It was a fertile time for great names: Coca-Cola was invented two years earlier. Eastman once explained how the name came to him:

I knew a trade name must be short, vigorous, incapable of being misspelled to an extent that it will destroy its identity, and in order to satisfy trademark laws it must mean nothing. The letter "k" had been a favourite with me; it seemed a strong, incisive sort of letter.

PHILIP KOTLER

One of the most famous MARKETING gurus, and author of the classic standard textbook *Marketing Management*.

Kotler has been something of a counterweight to the Theodore Levitt school of global marketing, arguing that markets are becoming more fragmented, not less. For instance, he has written:

*The heart of modern strategic marketing can be
described as STP marketing, namely segmenting,
targeting and positioning. This does not obviate
the importance of LGD marketing – lunch, golf
and dinner marketing – but rather provides the
broader framework for strategic success in the
marketplace. Today's companies are finding it
increasingly unrewarding to practice mass
marketing or product variety marketing. Mass
markets are becoming "demassified". They are
dissolving into hundreds of micromarkets.*

LAUNCH

The introduction of a new PRODUCT on to the MAR-
KET. This can be done in two ways: either with a
whimper or with a bang.

The whimper approach is to dribble the product on to a small part of the whole market in a sort
of test MARKETING; or to launch it nationally without
any ADVERTISING in the hope that word-of-mouth
will make it succeed. The latter approach worked
with the popular game Trivial Pursuit, but has
failed in many other instances.

Most big companies launch their new products
with a bang. This involves a co-ordinated ADVER-
TISING CAMPAIGN, special PROMOTION, and intensive
DISTRIBUTION.

Either lead, follow or get out of my way.
Sign on the desk of Ted Turner, founder of CNN

LEASING

A contractual arrangement in which the use of a
piece of equipment over a period of time is sold
by one party (the lessor) to another party (the
lessee).

Leasing rather than outright purchase is preferred by many companies because it reduces the
demand on their cash flow in the short term (there
is no capital outlay). It may also guarantee service
from the lessee (important in the case of complicated equipment). And it offers the prospect of
updating products on favourable terms.

LICENSING

Selling the right to use some process, trademark,
patent, and so on, in return for a fee or for the
payment of royalties. Licensing is a relatively low-
risk way of entering a foreign MARKET: the licensee
(the purchaser of the right) bears most of the risks
incurred. If the licensee is an effective marketer,
the licenser (the seller of the right) can reap a rich
reward for little risk.

Licensing is often used to enter markets where
direct entry is difficult; for example, in Japan or

eastern Europe. For example, Massey Ferguson gave a Polish company the right to manufacture its branded tractors.

> *Lada and Skoda sound as if they were both invented by the same communist preconception of what is a suitable name for a car. In fact, Emil Skoda was a pre-communist Czech engineer who founded the company in 1869; Lada is a Russian folk word meaning "beloved".*

LIFESTYLE

The way people choose to live, based on their ATTITUDE to life. Segmenting markets according to lifestyle is popular among researchers trying to classify groups of consumers in ways that relate to their behaviour in shops.

One such classification, developed by the Stanford Research Institute in the USA, is called Values and Lifestyles (VALS). It contains the following categories:

- **Belongers.** Patriotic, stable, sentimental traditionalists who are content with their lives.
- **Achievers.** Prosperous, self-assured, middle-aged materialists.
- **Emulators.** Ambitious young adults trying to break into the system.
- **I-am-me group.** Impulsive, experimental, a bit narcissistic.
- **Societally conscious.** Mature, successful, mission-oriented people who like causes.
- **Survivors.** The old and poor, with little optimism about the future.
- **Sustainers.** Resentful of their condition – one of trying to make ends meet.

Most consumers feel that they fall into several different VALS categories in their lifetimes.

There has been considerable interest in trying to decide whether there are lifestyles common to the whole of the European Union, and whether such lifestyles can be the basis of "single marketing to a single market". So far, research has come up with four "types" common to all west European countries, and a fifth that exists only in southern Europe: Greece, Italy, Portugal and Spain.

- **Successful idealists.** A group that is said to represent 5–15% of the population. These people are wealthy, but they are also into art, ecology and healthy eating.
- **Affluent materialists.** These are the BRAND-conscious, conspicuous consumers, usually representing some 15% of the population. They drive German cars, wear Italian suits and eat French cuisine.
- **Comfortable belongers.** The backbone of a nation, representing 25–50% of a population. These are the people who live in the suburbs and always vote for conservative policies.
- **Disaffected survivors.** These people are at the bottom of the pile, know it, and resent it. They are frequently unemployed and from ethnic minorities, and they account for as much as a quarter of the population.
- **Optimistic strivers.** A group that appears only in southern Europe, in transit from the soil to the suburbs. They are not yet comfortable belongers but they are getting there. They are young, ambitious, skilled and potentially affluent.

LIFETIME VALUE

A salutary reminder that in many industries the customer is not "here today; gone tomorrow". In banking, for instance, customers may continue to buy services from one institution throughout their life. The idea behind lifetime value (LTV) is that the return from an individual customer is not based on the profit from a single transaction, but rather from the whole series of transactions which that customer may make during his or her lifetime.

LINE EXTENSION

Increasing a PRODUCT LINE by adding variations of an existing BRAND. When a company has a successful brand there is a temptation to use the brand name on other products. Thus a well-known brand of hand lotion might have variants for dry skin, sensitive skin, detergent-damaged skin, and so on. One of the most successful extensions of recent years was the launch of the Mars bar in ice-cream form.

Line extension runs the risk of weakening the brand name. If the lotion for sensitive skin is no good, then the original lotion's IMAGE suffers. It also runs the risk of consumers substituting the new product for an old one: buying the new lotion instead of (not as well as) the old one.

LINE FILLING

Adding more products to an existing PRODUCT LINE in order to leave no gaps for competitors to move into. Procter & Gamble, a past master at line filling, has more than 20 brands of fabric-washing products. Each is differentiated in some way from the others.

When product lines are increased by moving UPMARKET or downmarket to attract new customers, the process is sometimes called line stretching. In the market for office photocopiers, the major manufacturers have stretched the line both upwards (to large high-speed multifunctional machines with sophisticated sorting capacity) and downwards to small machines that are low enough in price to be purchased for the home.

LIST BROKER

An organisation that gathers lists of names and addresses and sells them to marketers for DIRECT MARKETING. To some extent the broker can tailor lists according to the marketer's needs; for example, children under 15 living in households above a certain income level might be worth mailing for the launch of a new BRAND of expensive UPMARKET ice-cream. In the USA there are as many as 10,000 different lists available.

A secondary industry is that of using "de-duplication" computer programs to eliminate the duplication of names and addresses from a number of lists. The computer matches names and addresses on one disk with those on another, but it cannot cope with slight differences in postal codes or in the spelling of street names.

LOCALISATION

Originally this referred to the tendency of industries to stick together: jewellers in one district, lacemakers in another, hosiers in yet another.

In modern parlance localisation has come to have a very specific MARKETING meaning, the exact opposite of globalisation: ie, the tailoring of goods and services for small local markets, taking fully into account a market's geographical and cultural differences.

The debate between those marketers in favour of globalisation and those in favour of localisation has been resolved by the creation of the slogan: "Think global, act local". Even Procter & Gamble, which once believed that its great marketing prowess could brush aside all cultural differences, has now taken on board that it must account for local differences and must fine-tune its "world products" accordingly.

LOSS-LEADER

A retailing device whereby a particular PRODUCT is priced at a loss in order to "lead" customers into the shop. Once in the shop, the intention is that they should buy not only the loss-leader but also items on which the RETAILER makes a profit. Loss-leaders are often sold on a limited availability basis – "while stocks last" or "to the first 50 customers only".

Loss-leader PRICING is a device to promote the retail outlet and not the product, and there are plenty of manufacturers who are not happy for their products to be used as loss-leaders. Martini & Rossi, for example, has withheld supplies of its drinks from stores that have used them as loss-leaders.

LOW-INVOLVEMENT PRODUCT

A product that is purchased without much deliberation or forethought involving neither ego nor much money; in other words the type of product where a poor purchasing decision does not have very significant consequences.

The challenge for marketers is to try and make low-involvement products more interesting to consumers. Heavy ADVERTISING to develop BRAND LOYALTY is one device; for example, the old Lux soap advertisements that used to use film stars' endorsements. While soap is not something that consumers want to become involved with, film stars are.

LOYALTY CARD

The plastic card on which customer's LOYALTY POINTS are recorded electronically. Loyalty cards allow firms, such as supermarket chains, to track precisely their customers' behaviour, and this can be a useful guide for future business strategies.

LOYALTY POINTS

A way of retaining customers' loyalty to a product or service. "Points" related to the volume (or value) of the customer's purchase are recorded on a LOYALTY CARD. They can then be redeemed for goods or services (like holidays and hair-dryers), or, in the case of supermarkets, vouchers which can be used to pay for goods.

LTV

See LIFETIME VALUE.

Lego, the educational toy, is not Latin for "I read", but Danish for "play well" (leg godt). Its inventor was a Danish carpenter called Ole Kirk Christiansen.

M

Macro marketing

A term taken from economics that refers to MARKETING as studied in the context of large aggregations rather than of small units. Macro marketing is concerned with the flow of goods and services from producers to consumers within whole economic systems, and with the social processes that direct such flows.

Micro marketing is concerned with marketing processes in individual companies, and with individual consumer's and organisation's buying behaviour.

Madison Avenue

A main north–south street on Manhattan Island, New York, that used to be home to the head offices of all the world's biggest ADVERTISING agencies. Madison Avenue became synonymous with advertising much as Wall Street, in the south of Manhattan, is synonymous with banking and finance.

However, the industry has spread its wings in recent years. Not only are some of the biggest agencies now based in cities outside the USA, but some big US agencies have their major offices in places like Chicago and Los Angeles.

Mail order

The use of the mail service as a DISTRIBUTION CHANNEL to link the manufacturer, WHOLESALER and/or RETAILER directly with the consumer. Based on catalogue selling, mail order is a long-established business in the USA. Mail order is also strong in Germany through firms like Quelle and Otto Versand.

Mail order used to be considered a downmarket way of selling, but the growth of operations like Banana Republic in the USA and Next Directory in the UK has shown that it can be made to appeal to more UPMARKET consumers as well.

Many card companies (like American Express and MasterCard) also run mail-order businesses, sending catalogues in the mail along with their bills and statements. These companies are having to pay to send huge amounts of mail in any case.

They feel that they might as well put something else in their envelopes.

MAILSHOT
Printed material that is sent by mail to consumers in order to persuade them to purchase something.

MANUFACTURER BRAND
A BRAND that carries the name of the manufacturer, such as Kellogg, Kodak or Ford.

> *Shakespeare was wrong. A rose by any other name would not smell as sweet ... which is why the single most important decision in the marketing of perfume is the name.*
> Al Ries and Jack Trout

MARK-UP PRICING
A PRICING technique, widely used by retailers, whereby a PRODUCT's selling price is set by adding a certain percentage to its cost price (that is, marking it up).

MARKET
In MARKETING terms, a group of consumers who share some particular characteristic which affects their needs or wants, and which makes them potential buyers of a PRODUCT. For example:

● **The soap market.** All those people who share an enthusiasm for personal cleanliness.
● **The teenage market.** Anyone between their 13th and 20th birthday.
● **The housing market.** Everybody who wants a roof over their head.
● **The leisure market.** All those with spare time on their hands.
● **The US market.** Anybody who goes shopping in the United States.

The more tightly the market for a product can be defined, the easier it is to plan an effective MARKETING strategy.

M

MARKET RESEARCH

Sometimes called marketing research. The collection and analysis of information about consumers, markets and the effectiveness of MARKETING decisions. A study in the USA found that companies use market research for many different things including, in descending order of popularity:

- measurement of market potential;
- determination of market characteristics;
- MARKET SHARE analysis;
- sales analysis;
- studies of business trends;
- competitive PRODUCT studies;
- short-range forecasting (up to one year);
- new product acceptance and potential;
- long-range forecasting (more than one year);
- PRICING studies;
- testing of existing products;
- establishing of sales quotas and territories.

Most market research consists of making a survey of a particular sample of people by asking them to complete a QUESTIONNAIRE. This is usually done by personal interview, by post, or by telephone.

In research, the horizon recedes as we advance, and is no nearer at 60 than it was at 20. As the power of endurance weakens with age, the urgency of the pursuit grows more intense ... and research is always incomplete.
Mark Pattison (1813–84)

These surveys may be individual projects (called ad hoc research) carried out by a company's own market-research department, or by a market-research agency. Some surveys run by professional market-research firms use a regular panel of consumers or retail stores to keep a continuous eye on the movement of goods (see A.C. NIELSEN).

Market research is not limited to consumer and industrial markets. Politicians and social scientists also benefit from it, although when used for such purposes it is usually called "opinion polling" or "social research".

Market research has become a recognised profession in recent years; the Market Research Society (MRS) has some 5,000 members worldwide. It publishes a monthly newsletter and the more learned *Journal of the Market Research Society*.

> *Market research is like driving along looking in the rear-view mirror. You are studying what has gone.*
>
> Anita Roddick, founder of Body Shop

MARKET SEGMENTATION

It is generally more satisfactory to market products to a group of consumers who have similar characteristics, wants and needs than to the general, undifferentiated public. The match between what the consumer wants and what the manufacturer offers is then likely to be closer.

Groups of consumers with quite detailed characteristics in common are called "market segments", and the process of identifying them is called "market segmentation".

Markets may be segmented in many different ways, depending on the insight or perceptiveness of the marketer. Consumer market segments are commonly based on the following kinds of characteristics.

- **Demographic:** sheltered housing targeted at the over 60s; Ferrari cars for men with very high incomes.
- **Geographic:** country, state, region. A company may choose to sell its products in selected areas, or it may sell different products in different areas. Nestlé markets Nescafé in both the USA and the UK; but its decaffeinated freeze-dried Taster's Choice brand is not distributed in the UK. The company does, however, market a (different) decaffeinated coffee there.
- **Psychographic:** social class, LIFESTYLE, personality. Manufacturers of clothes, furniture, food prod-

ucts, cosmetics, drinks and cars give great attention to market segments based on these variables.

- **Use:** occasion, user status, user rate. There is a hot-drink-before-bedtime market, as well as a summer-barbecue market, a charter-flight market, a health-food market, and so on. There are potential user, first-time user and regular-user markets, and there are markets segmented into light, medium and heavy users.

Industrial markets are frequently segmented by type of organisation (such as manufacturing, governmental, agricultural) or by type of goods required (such as raw materials, installations, services).

A market segment must meet certain standards if it is to be the focus of a MARKETING effort.

- Its size and purchasing power must be substantial enough to promise a profitable return.
- It must be accessible.
- It must have future as well as present viability.

The meek shall inherit the earth, but they'll never increase market share.

William McGovan, ex-chairman of MCI

MARKET SHARE

A measure of a company's MARKETING success: its sales expressed as a percentage of total sales in a given market. Market share is looked on as a key indicator of competitive strength vis-à-vis rival companies.

One of the major differences between Japanese companies and companies in Europe and the USA is the degree of emphasis that they place on market share. For Japanese companies market share is at least as significant as profit; for western companies it is not.

Defining the boundaries of a market (in order to calculate market share) can be difficult. Is the market share for a firm's instant coffee to be calculated with respect to the sales of all instant coffee, or of all coffee, or of all hot drinks (including tea)? The significance of a company's market share depends critically on what market is being shared.

MARKETING

Officially defined as: "The management process responsible for identifying, anticipating and satisfying customer requirements profitably." Since non-profit organisations can also use marketing, the definition might be expanded to "those activities performed by individuals or organisations, whether profit or non-profit, that enable, facilitate and encourage exchange to take place to the satisfaction of both parties".

In *The Basic Arts of Marketing* Prabhu Guptara identifies six activities that come under the umbrella title of "marketing".

1 Identifying the needs of existing and potential customers (an emphasis on satisfying customer requirements is central to any definition of marketing)

2 Determining the best PRODUCT strategy.

3 Ensuring the effective DISTRIBUTION of products.

4 Informing customers of the existence of products and persuading them to buy those products.

5 Determining the prices at which products should be sold.

6 Ensuring that AFTER-SALES SERVICE is of the right QUALITY.

The function of satisfying customer requirements has become a major strategic focus for companies in recent years (the customer is king, again), resulting in much greater attention being given to the QUALITY of services and products.

Marketing is everything, and everything is marketing.
Regis McKenna

MARKETING AUDIT

There are two not unrelated meanings.

1 Extensive productivity analysis, a process that judges how well resources are being used in a company's MARKETING DEPARTMENT. In this context the term is used in an accounting sense; it is an investigation enabling the auditor to draw conclusions about the stewardship of the marketing management.

2 One of the critical steps in the planning process, in which the existing marketing situation and the company's marketing capability are assessed.

MARKETING BUDGET

A financial statement about the level of MARKETING effort to be undertaken by a company. The marketing budget represents the cost of achieving the company's marketing objectives as described in the MARKETING PLAN.

The budget is expressed as a profit and loss statement, showing both the revenues anticipated from sales and the costs of the marketing resources that will be put into the MARKETING MIX.

Not everything that goes by the name "marketing" deserves it. It has become too fashionable. A grave-digger remains a grave-digger even when called a mortician; only the cost of the burial goes up.
Peter Drucker

MARKETING DEPARTMENT

The department in a company that is responsible for MARKETING; to some extent its size and form depend on the size and nature of the company (whether it is in consumer goods or INDUSTRIAL GOODS, and so on).

In a not untypical company the director of marketing will answer to the managing director, and will have various divisions under him or her:

- for ADVERTISING and sales PROMOTION;
- for sales;
- for MARKET RESEARCH;
- for PRODUCT planning;
- for administration.

Marketing flop

About 80% of all new products never become commercial successes. An enterprising Scot, Robert McMath, opened a "product museum" in Naples, New York, where some of these failures have been saved from total oblivion. They include the following.

- Touch of yoghurt shampoo.
- Gorilla Balls vitamin-enriched malt candy.
- Nullo deodorant tablets.
- Northwoods Egg Coffee.
- Male Chauvinist "awfully arrogant" aftershave.

All of them represent pain and disappointment to some unknown small entrepreneur. But the mighty make mistakes too, and their failures often become more famous. Ford offered its large and powerful Edsel to a MARKET that wanted smaller economic cars. And Coca Cola's decision in the early 1990s to produce a new-taste Coke for a market used to and happy with the existing taste proved an expensive and embarrassing mistake.

Before the war he was an alert, hard-hitting aggressive marketing executive. As such, he was a very bad marketing executive. Colonel Cargill was so awful a marketing executive that his services were much sought after by firms eager to establish losses for tax purposes.
Joseph Heller, *Catch 22*

Marketing management

One of the four main management functions in a company along with production management, financial management and R&D.

There are nine widely recognised responsibilities of marketing management.

1 Finding out the facts (MARKET RESEARCH).
2 Making predictions from research (forecasting).
3 Putting into effect changes arising from research (NEW PRODUCT DEVELOPMENT).

4 Making sure they are products that customers want to buy (BRAND MANAGEMENT).

5 Deciding on quantities (budgeting).

6 Deciding at what price goods should be sold and for what profit (PRICING policy).

7 Moving goods from their point of manufacture to their point of consumption (DISTRIBUTION).

8 Selling (sales management).

9 Persuading through communication (ADVERTISING).

MARKETING MIX

A description of the various elements of the MARKETING process that must be co-ordinated to make up the total marketing effort. These elements are often crudely summarised as the Four Ps.

1 PRODUCT. What product is going to be offered to the customer? What are its characteristics; its BRAND name; its PACKAGING? What additions can be made to the PRODUCT LINE?

2 Price. How much is the customer going to pay for the product? How are price levels to be adjusted in the light of consumers' responses and of competitors' behaviour?

3 Place. How is the product going to get to where the customer is when the customer wants it? What type of wholesale and retail outlets are to be used? What is to be the geographical coverage? What sales force is needed and what will be its size, territories and style of selling?

4 PROMOTION. How is the customer going to know about the product, and be persuaded to buy it? What ADVERTISING is to be used and what will be its nature, content, frequency and reach? How much sales promotion, publicity and personal selling are there to be?

To reflect many companies' growing customer-orientation, there is a tendency to refer less to the Four Ps, and more to the Four Cs.

1 Customer value. (From the buyer's point of view.) This replaces product.

2 Cost to the customer. This is more than the price charged because it includes the cost of the customer's time and energy; it replaces price.

3 Convenience for the buyer. This replaces place.

4 Communication. This is a dialogue which replaces promotion (a monologue by the seller).

Marketing is just sales with a college education.
Anon

MARKETING PLAN

The plan drawn up by managers of products, brands or markets to define their objectives and strategies. Typically, a marketing plan will consist of the following sections.

● An analysis of past MARKETING performance, with data on the relevant MARKET (size, growth, consumer behaviour, trends); the PRODUCT (sales, prices, profits); the competition (size, MARKET SHARE, strategies); DISTRIBUTION and the environment (demographic, economic, political and technological trends).

This leads to a statement on the company's strengths and weaknesses and the opportunities and threats facing it.

● The formulation of marketing objectives, in relation to financial objectives (profits, sales revenues, return on capital, and so on). The marketing objectives might be to increase the PRODUCT LINE's market share by 3% over the planning period, or to increase the sales revenue of the BRAND by 5%. Whenever possible marketing objectives are stated quantitatively, with a given time period for their achievement.

● The development of marketing strategies. For each objective, managers have to decide which of many possible strategies to follow. If the aim is to increase the product line's market share, a brand might be selected for increased marketing support, or another brand might be added to the line. The brand's sales revenues might be increased by using a special sales PROMOTION. Or the price of the brand might be raised.

● The preparation of action plans setting out what is to be done, who will do it, when and at what cost.

MASS COMMUNICATION

An old-fashioned term for the use of the mass MEDIA (nationwide newspapers, radio and television) for communicating with an audience.

MASS MARKET

The opposite of a segmented market (see MARKET SEGMENTATION); the market in its entirety. Fewer and fewer products are expected to appeal to a mass market, so fewer and fewer products need MASS COMMUNICATION.

> *It's just called The Bible now. We dropped the word Holy to give it more mass-market appeal.*
> Spokesperson, Hodder & Stoughton, publishers

ME TOO

A PRODUCT modelled consciously on a successful competitor: the type of product that appears on a MARKET with no differentiating features from already-existing products. Me too products can be seen as an indication of the successful MARKETING of the products being copied.

Such products usually have a short life and are quickly forgotten. Sometimes they are produced by well-known companies. Cadbury's Aztec bar was meant to be an answer to the Mars bar, but it turned out to be much too similar. With no special character of its own, it flopped.

MEDIA

The vehicles that carry ADVERTISING (among other things): for example, television, radio, newspapers, magazines, billboards and posters. The mass media are those vehicles which reach a national audience.

MEDIA ANALYSIS

The study of the effectiveness of various MEDIA in reaching an audience. Finding answers to questions like:

- How many people who buy a magazine look at the back cover, the inside front cover, the centre-spread, and so on?
- How many people driving past a BILLBOARD at 100kph can read print 2 metres high?
- How many people stay awake long enough to see the credits to the late-night movie?

Freedom of the press is freedom to print such of the proprietor's prejudices as the advertisers don't object to.
Hannen Swaffer

MEDIA BROKER

An agency that buys MEDIA space (air-time, magazine pages, and so on) "in bulk" from a television station or a publisher. The broker then sells the space to a number of clients in smaller bits. This practice grew first in countries like France that are dominated by a small number of powerful media groups, but it has spread widely as a way of exploiting economies of scale. Some of the biggest media brokers are owned by ADVERTISING agencies, eager to redress what they see as an imbalance of power between their clients and the media barons.

MEDIA BUYING

The purchasing of time or space in MEDIA for the showing of advertisements. This task is usually delegated to a specialist "media buyer" inside each ADVERTISING AGENCY. However, more and more specialist companies are setting up as "media buyers". Their services are then used by advertising agencies that do not have their own media departments.

In recent years a number of advertising agencies have pooled their media-buying departments. This has been done in order to enable them to buy space (or time) in even bigger bulk from newspapers and radio or television stations. Through the even bigger discounts that this gives them, they reap further economies of scale.

One danger in all this is that individual agencies reveal more than they wish to other agencies about the media-buying strategies of their clients.

MEDIA PLAN

The decisions made by advertisers about which MEDIA to use for an ADVERTISING CAMPAIGN. This is a question of making the most effective use of each medium within the limits of the media budget.

Media planners must know how best to reach their target audience: which magazines or newspapers such and such an audience reads, which television programmes they watch, and so on. They must then work out the percentage of the target market that they hope will see the campaign; the number of times during the campaign they want each of those people to see it; and the cost of reaching them (see CPM).

MERCHANDISING

A smart term for selling. In some industries (like the rag trade) sales people are called merchandisers. Merchandising implies rather more than selling: unlike selling, it is not, for example, done door-to-door. Merchandising involves the whole range of activities that can be used to increase the sale of goods through retail outlets.

MICRO MARKETING

See MACRO MARKETING.

MIDDLEMAN

Anyone who lies on the DISTRIBUTION CHANNEL between a manufacturer and a consumer. In the remorseless drive to cut costs, most industries have attempted to eliminate the middleman as much as possible.

MILKING

A short-sighted MARKETING strategy that aims to

make as much profit from a PRODUCT in as short a time as possible, with no regard to the long-term future of the product. This is often an appropriate strategy for marketing a FAD like toys, dolls and various accessories.

3M – the Minnesota Mining and Manufacturing Company – is a misnomer. 3M has done scarcely any mining this century. And it is more famous for its "Scotch" tape than for anything in Minnesota.

MILLENIUM BOMB

When computers were first produced their memories were limited. So everything was done to avoid overloading them with unnecessary information. That included removing the digits '19' from the beginning of references to current years. Hence many older generation computers contain the seeds of an enormous problem when we switch to a new century. At 00.01 hours on January 1st 2000 these computers will think that Queen Victoria is still on the throne.

Why does that matter? Well, for example, it will confuse programs that calculate the interest due on a late payment. A creditor owed 18 months interest on a debt at the turn of the century will be recorded as not being owed anything for ninety-eight and a half years.

From noodles to atomic power.
Slogan of Mitsubishi

MISSIONARY SELLING

A technique used by a company to support its WHOLESALER'S or distributor's sales force. A publisher's representative (the missionary SALES PERSON) might, for example, visit teachers in order to inform them of new books that the publisher is bringing out in their field. The teachers in turn recommend the books to their students. The students then buy them from nearby bookshops which have purchased their stock from the distributor's sales representative.

MOTHER-IN-LAW RESEARCH

The sort of MARKET RESEARCH that involves asking questions casually of a few friends, colleagues and family, including your mother-in-law. Useful when wishing to confirm pre-conceived attitudes.

MOTIVATIONAL RESEARCH

A form of MARKET RESEARCH popularised by Ernest Dichter. Using techniques like word association, sentence completion and ink-blot interpretation, he tried to discover consumers' underlying attitudes towards products.

Motivational research into air travel led advertisers to emphasise its time-saving aspects rather than its safety, since an appeal to safety merely aroused people's irrational fear of flying.

Research into consumer attitudes to prunes revealed that their shrunken, wrinkled appearance reminded people of old age. The MARKETING solution to this problem for prune producers in the USA was to launch a new PRODUCT: bottled prune juice.

MULTI-BRAND STRATEGY

The practice of carrying many brands within one PRODUCT LINE; a strategy developed and practised by Procter & Gamble with, for example, its 24 different brands of fabric-washing products.

The strategy has several objectives.

● It is a means of obtaining greater shelf space in retail outlets, relative to competitors.
● It is a way of dealing with "BRAND switchers", customers who like to try a different brand from time to time.
● It is a way of dealing with would-be competitors, leaving them no gaps in the market.
● It is a way of segmenting the market, providing brands which may develop their own loyal followers.
● It is a strategy that can be used to create a de-

gree of competition among a company's brand managers, and to keep them on their toes.

MULTI-DIMENSIONAL SCALING

A MARKET RESEARCH technique to measure ATTITUDE. People's attitudes, including their tastes, feelings and opinions, are complex; any attempt to define them, therefore, must use a many-sided (multi-dimensional) approach.

Market researchers use scales to measure different degrees of attitude, such as the Likert Scale and the Semantic Differential Scale. In the Likert system the respondent simply chooses the word or words which best describe his or her feelings towards the object being tested, and the choice is recorded on a scale of one to five. For example:

Q. Do you like yoghurt?
A. Dislike extremely (1); dislike (2); neutral (3); like (4); like extremely (5).

The Semantic Differential technique uses several questions about the PRODUCT, each with a number of possible answers from negative to positive values (from –2 to +2). The number values of the respondent's answers are added together to give a sum which represents his or her "net" attitude to the product.

MULTIPLE

One of a large chain of stores, the type of stores that appear on all of a nation's major high streets.

RALPH NADER

The pioneer of the consumer movement in the USA, once described as being "like a virgin in a whorehouse". Nader fought and won many legal battles on behalf of consumers who had suffered because of faulty products.

The consumer movement in the USA (and likewise in Europe) came about in a confrontational way. Consumers lived through a series of High Noon-style showdowns with producers.

Keep in mind the fact that Ralph Nader could be the first customer for your new product.

Anon

NATIONAL LAUNCH

The method of introducing a new PRODUCT into a MARKET by making it available throughout the entire market at one time rather than by distributing it gradually, area by area. (See also LAUNCH.)

NETWORK MARKETING

A method of selling that is, basically, a way of taking the well-known "Tupperware party" formula to the streets. Particularly appropriate for selling costume jewellery, one practitioner described network marketing as having three essential elements.

1 The SALES PERSON wears the PRODUCT.
2 He or she carries the catalogue with them.
3 He or she talks about the business everywhere and all the time.

This practitioner claims to have sold jewellery this way at a supermarket checkout and in a doctor's waiting room.

NEW PRODUCT DEVELOPMENT

The range of activities involved in conceiving, developing and launching a new PRODUCT into a MARKET. New product development (NPD) is a critically important process since most firms introduce new products frequently and continually in order to retain competitive advantage.

Failure rates are high. Only about half the new products launched on the market become commercially viable, and only one in 40 new product ideas ever becomes a successful product.

Nestlé's trademark of birds in a nest was designed by Henri Nestlé himself, a research chemist who started the Swiss food company in 1866. (In Swiss-German Nestlé means little nest.)

NICHE MARKETING
The fashionable idea of selling a product or service to a small, narrowly defined market. Originally known as CONCENTRATED SEGMENTATION.

A.C. NIELSEN
A US company founded in 1939 and now the most famous MARKET-RESEARCH firm in the world. Its services include the well-known Nielsen Index, a measure of shopping patterns established by a continuous monitoring of sales from retail food outlets, drug stores/chemists, liquor stores and CASH-AND-CARRY wholesalers. In the USA Nielsen is also well known for its measurement of the size of television audiences.

NON-PROFIT MARKETING
The application of MARKETING to the non-profit sector. Symphony orchestras, art galleries, universities and the armed forces are not usually in the business of seeking profits. But they are in a relationship with the public, and to nourish that relationship they need to use marketing techniques. Hence museums run shops; the armed forces advertise for recruits.

NPD
See NEW PRODUCT DEVELOPMENT.

ODD-EVEN PRICING

A PRICING convention used in retailing whereby a PRODUCT's price is not rounded up, but left as a figure ending (usually) in a five or a nine (both "odd" numbers). Thus 99p is used in preference to £1; and $24.95 in preference to $25.

This odd convention persists even though it has never been proved that consumers actually think, or even feel, that "odd" priced goods are better value than "even" priced goods.

OFF-THE-PEG RESEARCH

MARKET RESEARCH that uses old data collected by someone other than the researcher. The four main types of material taken off-the peg are:

- published sources;
- data regularly collected and sold by market research companies (see SYNDICATED RESEARCH);
- data on specialist subjects regularly collected and sold by market research companies (see under SPECIALIST RESEARCH);
- data commissioned from syndicated surveys (see OMNIBUS RESEARCH).

OFF-CARD RATE

The selling of ADVERTISING space in a newspaper, or of time on a television channel, at a price below that quoted on the medium's RATE CARD.

OMNIBUS RESEARCH

The results of surveys that are based on questionnaires sent out regularly to a panel of respondents by market researchers. Space on the QUESTIONNAIRE is sold and made available to firms which have specific MARKET-RESEARCH needs.

This practice is called "omnibus" research because it carries a number of different passengers.

ONE-STOP SHOPPING

A strategy once fashionable among service firms based on a belief that customers like to buy services as they buy groceries: all in one place. Groups like SAATCHI & SAATCHI believed that clients who popped in for a spot of ADVERTISING might also buy, say, a bit of MARKET RESEARCH and a human-resources consultant while they were on the premises.

OPEN-ENDED QUESTION

A question that requires a longer answer than "yes", "no" or "don't know". For example:

- What features do you look for in considering the purchase of a new car?
- What factors do you think are important in preparing meals for your family?

OPINION LEADER

A person who influences the purchasing behaviour of others, often by word of mouth or example. Opinion leaders are not necessarily the first to adopt a new PRODUCT or idea (see INNOVATOR), but their acceptance of it is vitally important to its ultimate success.

If these people can be reached by selected media advertising, then the multiplier effect widens public acceptance of the product very efficiently.

I could prove God, statistically.
George Gallup

OPINION POLL

Consumer research concerned specifically with politics. Opinion polls are now an integral part of political campaigns in most parts of the world. The polls are usually commissioned by the MEDIA (newspapers, and so on) for consumption by the public, but political parties themselves also commission opinion polls to help them with their campaign strategies.

Some market research agencies have become famous for their opinion polling – firms like Gallup, Harris and MORI. They use various techniques, from telephone calls to face-to-face interviews, and work with samples that are rarely larger than a couple of thousand. Their ability to predict electoral outcomes is unpredictable.

OPTIMISTIC STRIVER
A type of consumer found particularly in southern Europe: Greece, Italy, Portugal and Spain (see LIFESTYLE).

ORANGE GOODS
A category of consumer goods – including things like clothing – that consumers change at a moderate rate, either because of wear-and-tear or because of changing fashion. Orange goods are to be contrasted with FAST-MOVING CONSUMER GOODS where the turnover is much quicker.

ORGANISATIONAL BUYING
The way in which organisations, as opposed to individuals, identify, evaluate and choose the products that they buy.

A car manufacturer, for example, buys hundreds of components from accessory suppliers. The company's negotiations with such suppliers may start at the early stages of the development of a new model, and it may then continue right through until that model is removed from the market.

OVERKILL
An intensive MARKETING effort that produces diminishing returns because it engenders a hostile rather than a favourable reaction among consumers.

OWN LABEL
See DEALER BRAND.

PACKAGED GOODS

Consumer goods that are packaged by their manufacturer, and not sold loose. Such goods include most food, cosmetics and cleaning products. Despite the advantages of packaged goods (for hygiene, for example), many consumers still seek out unpackaged alternatives; of fruit and vegetables in particular, and of sweets.

PACKAGING

The wrapping in which goods are presented for sale. The packaging of many products has become an integral part of the PRODUCT itself. Originally designed to protect the product, it now carries out a range of other functions as well. It may be:

- A convenient means for dispensing its contents (liquid soaps, glue or toothpaste, for example).
- A means for carrying key information about the contents (sometimes required by law).
- An important means for promoting and ADVERTISING the product itself. People may still wish to buy boiled sweets in brown paper bags, but they want their designer chocolates in something a bit more glamorous.

PAIRED COMPARISONS

A technique used in MARKET RESEARCH. It asks consumers to rank their preferences among different products. They are presented with a pair of products or brands and asked to choose the one they prefer. Soft-drink research might use the following pairs.

Coca-Cola–Pepsi Cola	Pepsi-Cola–7 Up
Coca Cola–7 Up	Pepsi-Cola–Dr Pepper
Coca-Cola–Dr Pepper	7 Up–Dr Pepper

The results will show the number of times that each brand is preferred in comparison with another. Coca-Cola, for example, might be preferred in every pairing and receive a rating of three, Pepsi might be preferred in two of the pairings. The final figures reveal an order of brand preference.

PANEL

A sample of consumers who record their purchases over time for the purposes of MARKET RESEARCH (see DIARY PANEL). Audits attempt to measure consumer patterns from the viewpoint of the seller; panels attempt to measure consumer patterns from the viewpoint of the buyer. The picture is rarely the same.

PARETO PRINCIPLE

Sometimes referred to as the 80/20 rule, the Pareto Principle is the observation of a common occurrence: that 80% of one thing comes from 20% of another. For example, many companies seem to derive 80% of their profits from 20% of their PRODUCT LINE; many sell 80% of their output through 20% of their DISTRIBUTION outlets.

The principle was first enunciated by a 19th-century Italian economist by the name of Pareto. But he first applied it to the wealth of nations, finding that 80% of the wealth belonged to 20% of the population, regardless of the absolute wealth of the nation. From that he concluded that the only way to spread wealth was to redistribute it; creating more of it would simply retain the same 80/20 ownership ratio.

20% of any group of salesmen will always produce 90% of the sales.

Robert Townsend's version of the Pareto principle, quoted in *Up the Organisation*

PATCHWORK PRODUCT

A PRODUCT which has so many problems that no sooner is one resolved than another appears.

PATENT

A type of protection for intellectual property. Registered patents protect inventions from being copied. Big companies heavily dependent on R&D, like pharmaceuticals firms and consumer-electronics manufacturers, own literally thousands of patents that they have registered with various authorities around the world.

PAYMENT SYSTEM

An increasingly important part of the selling process is the provision of suitable payment terms and conditions. Electronic payment systems have helped speed up progress through the SUPERMARKET checkout, and laser technology has helped produce detailed invoices, fast.

This is particularly helpful in the sale of fast-moving consumer goods. For consumer durables that are purchased only occasionally, much more important is the availability of facilities like hire purchase. For regular but infrequent purchases (like magazine subscriptions) techniques like the negative option (which continues a subscription into the next period unless the customer says "no") ease the purchasing process.

PENETRATION

The percentage of a TARGET MARKET that has bought a particular PRODUCT at least once.

PENETRATION STRATEGY

The use of low prices and heavy ADVERTISING to increase MARKET SHARE. Such a strategy is appropriate when a company has a PRODUCT in a MARKET which is being supplied with products that are relatively similar to one another.

For such a strategy to be attempted, a market will have to be large enough for the company to be able to sustain relatively low profit margins. The strategy has the added advantage that it may deter potential new entrants. They will be put off by a market that seems to have such limited possibilities for profit.

PERCEPTION

The process by which an individual receives, selects and interprets information. Marketers and ADVERTISING specialists are very interested in the phenomenon of perception; they want to find signals that will produce in the consumer a favourable view or perception of their PRODUCT (its IMAGE).

PERCEPTUAL MAPPING

A technique borrowed from psychology that helps marketers to understand the structure of a MARKET. Consumers develop an IMAGE of a PRODUCT based on its particular features, or its benefits (real or imagined), or its price. These perceptions can be identified (see QUALITATIVE RESEARCH) and products can then be plotted on a graph or map. The closer two brands are on the map, the closer they are competitively.

If research has also identified the characteristics of an "ideal" product, then the closer a brand is to that point, the more likely it is to be preferred over others. Gaps on the map may represent potential market opportunities.

PERSONAL SELLING

Direct face-to-face communication between a buyer and a seller. Personal selling is as old as MARKETING itself (see DIRECT MARKETING). In marketing INDUSTRIAL GOODS it is generally more important than ADVERTISING, because of the need for the SALES PERSON to meet the particular (and perhaps unique) requirements of each customer.

PIGGY BACKING

An expression used in DIRECT MARKETING to refer to the practice of placing direct marketing material into other businesses' envelopes – for example, a special offer on cookers slipped in with an electricity bill, or a mail-order catalogue folded with a credit-card bill and statement.

PILOT

A trial undertaken on a modest scale in order to test the feasibility of something much bigger. Thus a pilot plant is a small production operation set up to test new processes before a complete factory is commissioned. Likewise a pilot QUESTIONNAIRE is used in tests before being honed into a full MARKET-RESEARCH survey.

PITCH

As in "make a pitch" – to make a presentation in

the hope of winning a contract. A pitch is also the physical space where a street trader sells his wares.

PIMS
See PROFIT IMPACT OF MARKET STRATEGY.

POINT OF SALE
The place where the whole MARKETING effort culminates. The term usually refers to a retail store, but with the advent of self-service and the technological revolution, it may now mean a telephone call or a through-the-wall teller machine.

Increasingly, the point of sale is inside the customer's own home. Via so-called "home shopping" customers can make purchases in their pyjamas, by using the INTERNET or by following instructions on their television screens.

He who has a thing to sell
And goes and whispers in a well
Is not so apt to get the dollars
As he who climbs a tree and hollers.

Anon

PORTFOLIO ANALYSIS
A concept borrowed from the investment community, and now used by marketers as a way to evaluate a company's products in order to decide how best to allocate resources among them.

There are several different methods of product portfolio analysis in current use. All involve an analysis of the profitability, prospects and investment requirements of a company's products.

An ideal product mix consists of a balance between products which are very profitable and those which are expected to become very profitable. The cash coming in from the former is available for investment in support of the latter.

Portfolio analysis can be applied at many different levels of a business. In a large multi-product company it is applied at top-management level to the company's strategic business units (separate divisions, each of which handles one of the company's product lines). Then within each strategic business unit, portfolio analysis can be further applied by managers to analyse the specific products under their responsibility.

POSITIONING

The attempt by marketers to give a PRODUCT a certain identity or IMAGE that will help it to be perceived as having distinctive features or benefits.

A shopper set on buying a brand of dishwashing detergent that is kind to the hands is likely to choose Ivory Liquid in the USA, and Fairy Liquid in the UK. These are the products that are firmly positioned, vis-à-vis the shopper, in the "gentle to-hands" position.

If the shopper had wanted a simple, functional detergent at a cheap price then he or she would probably have plumped for the supermarket's own brand. Dealer brands hold the "reliable and cheaper" position in the market.

But suppose there is another brand of washing-up liquid on the shelf called Wash-up. Its label says it is kind to hands, and it is competitive in price. But the brand name does not mean these things to the consumer.

If the marketers of Wash-up do not want to see their product fail they must "position" it. They have two choices.

1 Because they know Wash-up is chemically gentle to hands they can try to implant the name Wash-up in the minds of consumers as being such, in direct competition with Ivory or Fairy.

The chances of success with this strategy are slim. Once a consumer has associated one brand name with a position, the bonding tends to last, to the effective exclusion of all others.

2 Alternatively, Wash-up's marketers are more likely to be successful if they can find a position in the market that no other brand has. They might discover, for example, that changing lifestyles have created an unfilled "masculine" position for the man-about-the-house who also cleans the pots. Their MARKETING efforts would then all be directed at creating a washing-up liquid for men.

In some markets almost every conceivable "position" seems to have been taken. With shampoos, for example, there are shampoos for dry hair, greasy hair, frequently washed hair, fair hair, dark hair, grey hair, baby hair, and so on.

POSTER

An ADVERTISING medium that forms a striking part of the landscape of most modern cities, although it accounts for less than 10% of all advertising expenditure.

Smaller posters are usually printed on paper and pasted on to visible parts of buildings. Larger posters are stuck on freestanding sites (called supersites) created especially for the purpose and usually located by the side of major highways. In the USA these are called billboards; in the UK they are known as hoardings (see BILLBOARD).

In some cases posters have developed into an art form. One Sony poster advertising its Walkman was so popular that (much to Sony's fury) it was simply removed from most public sites as a collector's item.

In some cities it is common to see whole sides of multi-storey apartment blocks covered with a single advertisement that attracts attention by its scale. In other large cities posters sometimes become like mobile sculptures, using real samples of the advertised product to attract attention.

The number of poster sites varies greatly in different countries. In France they are very popular, covering every pissoir and kiosk in sight. There are more than 575,000 poster sites in the country, compared with just over 100,000 in Italy and the UK.

PR

See PUBLIC RELATIONS.

PREDATORY PRICING

The practice of cutting prices with the specific intention of stealing market share from the competition. Thus a product's price may be cut to the bone in markets where its major competitor is strong, while being maintained at a higher level in markets where the competition is weak.

PREMIUM OFFER

A form of sales promotion that offers a customer the opportunity to obtain one PRODUCT, either free or at an attractive price, by purchasing another. It is a device that is particularly popular with cosmetics manufacturers; purchasers of a new aftershave, for example, can sometimes walk away from the shop with a piece of luggage or a towel that dwarfs their genuine purchase.

PRE-TESTING

A MARKET RESEARCH technique used to predict the effectiveness of an advertisement before it is (expensively) released. An ADVERTISING AGENCY will define the objectives of a piece of MEDIA advertising and then test it, using GROUP DISCUSSION, to determine the extent to which the objectives can expect to be realised.

Print advertising is sometimes tested by split runs, in which different advertisements are alternated and readers' responses to each are measured and compared.

The Schwerin test is a recognised method used in the USA to test television and radio commercials. Before being exposed to the commercial, respondents are asked to choose a brand. After seeing the advertisement they are asked to choose again; any change in their selection is considered to be a measure of the effectiveness of the commercial.

PRICE DISCRIMINATION

When intermediaries or industrial buyers purchase products of similar QUALITY (and in similar quantity) they expect to buy them on the same terms. If the seller favours one or more of its customers, and the difference in price cannot be justified in cost terms, then by law in the USA an offence has been committed.

This is not usually the case in other countries where, for example, a professional firm of builders will usually obtain lower prices from a builders' merchant than will an odd-job home-builder.

PRICE RING

A cartel of producers who fix prices among themselves. The best-known example is probably the oil-producing members of OPEC. But the big British clearing banks also once ran a price ring. They used to fix interest rates among themselves by agreeing in a series of clandestine telephone calls what rates should be.

PRICE SENSITIVE

The effect that an increase (or decrease) in price has on the sales of a PRODUCT or service. A product is said to be "highly price sensitive" if a small change in price results in a large change in sales. In general, low-price, commodity-type goods are very price sensitive; high-price, luxury goods are not.

PRICE WAR

The situation where firms try to gain MARKET SHARE by cutting their prices below those of their competitors. If the competitors follow suit this can lead to a vicious spiral in which many firms lose money, and some go bankrupt. To avoid this, some manufacturers fix (for their own internal purposes) a rock-bottom price which they vow they will never go below, even in the most bitter price war.

Airlines in the USA and holiday package-tour operators in the UK are notorious for engaging in price wars. Not entirely coincidentally, both industries have also seen more than their fair share of bankruptcies.

PRICING

The crucial art of deciding what price to charge for a PRODUCT or service. Set it too high and nobody will buy; set it too low and it is not worth the candle. (See also MILKING.)

There are as many ways to determine prices as there are to skin a cat. One is to add the fixed costs per unit to the variable costs per unit, and then to add a percentage for the profit. But this is a crude method, especially since the fixed cost per unit has to be guesswork. It cannot be known until the manufacturer knows how many units will be sold, and that cannot be known until the price has been fixed.

If the market allows, a simpler way to determine price is to follow the price leader: the market participant who "leads" prices up and down. The newcomer needs to follow a discrete distance behind the market leader, and with a price that is competitively lower.

In certain industries manufacturers are given "pricing points" that they have to stay below if they are to get the business at all. For example, a fashion retailer will decide that a certain type and style of blouse will sell at $29.95 and no more. The retailer works backwards from that amount, subtracting the profit and value-added at each stage in the manufacturing and distribution process in order to arrive at a pricing point for the manufacturer.

PRIME TIME

That time of day (or night) when there are most viewers watching television or listening to the radio. The MEDIA charge extra for advertisements that want to be shown in prime time.

Prime time on television is usually in the early evening; in the UK between 18.00 and 22.30. On commercial radio, though, prime time is often in the morning during breakfast.

PRIVATE LABEL

See DEALER BRAND.

PRIZE DRAW

A much-used device in direct mail offers whereby recipients who respond get their names (or rather their special numbers) entered into a draw for a car, a large amount of money or whatever. Although respondents must have by law the same chance of winning if they decline rather than accept the offer, it is clear that many of them do not realise this or do not believe it.

PRODUCT
Anything that can be offered to a MARKET that might satisfy a need or a want. It may be an object, a service, a place, an organisation, or an idea.

Products can be thought about on three levels.

● Every product has a core benefit (for example, soaps and detergents make things clean). This is known as "the core product".
● Products also have BRAND names, PACKAGING, QUALITY and style.
● Beyond these direct attributes there is the "augmented product", which includes guarantees, AFTER-SALES SERVICE, installation, delivery, credit terms, and so on.

PRODUCT CLASS
A term applied to a large grouping of products that have similar functions. Cigarettes, automobiles and microcomputers are each examples of a product class.

PRODUCT DIFFERENTIATION
The practice of making one PRODUCT distinguishable from others. Products may be differentiated by QUALITY, price, styling and service. In virtually every product class there are many products seeking to be differentiated from each other.

PRODUCT ELIMINATION
The orderly process of withdrawing a PRODUCT from the MARKET (also called product deletion). Products do not live forever. For most of them profitable life is short; even the most long-lived products can eventually go into decline.

Many companies do not like to face this fact. Through poor management or nostalgia they often keep products on offer even when they are consistently losing money. An unprofitable product is not necessarily an overall liability, however. In some cases it may contribute to the ease of selling other products. Car dealers, for example, may consider their reputations for excellent service are enhanced by stocking accessories for non-current models, products that in themselves are unprofitable to the manufacturer.

Products that have been marked for deletion, if they have been familiar brands, may be harvested, that is to say, they may be made to produce a short-term profit before they are withdrawn.

PRODUCT LIFE CYCLE

A concept that has attracted marketers for many years – the use of a biological analogy for products: they are born, introduced to the MARKET (in a sort of product bar-mitzvah), they grow in sales, mature (sales growth stops), and then they decline (sales fall off).

The analogy is sometimes extended also to markets; they too are born, grow and die, in what is referred to as a "demand life cycle".

It is tempting to deduce from this that it is possible to predict movements in sales according to the "time of life" of a particular product. Different marketing strategies can thus be developed for different stages in a product's life cycle.

Critics of the life-cycle approach argue that the shape of the sales curve, far from being pre-ordained, is a function of the marketing effort that is put into the product: hence the life cycle has no value as a forecasting tool.

Furthermore, critics point to brands which appear to demonstrate no life cycle. (Indeed, *The Economist* itself is one example. Born in 1843 it has been through several cycles in its 150-year history, none of them yet ending in anything like product elimination.)

The following table lists companies that were number one in their respective product classes in the USA in 1933, and were still number one more than 60 years later.

Company	Product
Campbell's	Soup
Coca-Cola	Soft drinks
Del Monte	Canned fruit
Eastman Kodak	Cameras, film
Gillette	Razors
Ivory	Soap
Nabisco	Biscuits
Wrigley	Chewing gum

Source: Interbrand.

PRODUCT LINE

A group of closely-related products marketed by the same company. Companies can have one or many product lines; and product lines can contain few or many products. Heinz has a product line with more than 57 varieties, while Procter & Gamble has something like 57 product lines. These include beauty care products, chemicals, detergents and disposable nappies.

The number of products within a product line is related to the number of different consumer segments that a company has been able to identify and supply.

PRODUCT MANAGEMENT

See BRAND MANAGEMENT.

PRODUCT MARKET

A company's PRODUCT LINE is frequently sold to several different classes of customer. Each of these classes (or "product markets") has distinct requirements. A line of food products, for example, may be sold to the retail market (grocery outlets), to the catering market (restaurants and hotels), and to the institutional market (schools, hospitals, military installations, or prisons). Each product market requires a different MARKETING approach.

PRODUCT MIX

This is the whole range of products offered to consumers by a single company. The product mix is described in the following terms.

- **Width.** The number of product lines that a company offers.
- **Length.** The number of brands of each product.
- **Depth.** The number of variants that each BRAND has; soap may come in hand size, bath size, guest size, family size, and so on.
- **Consistency.** The extent to which the product lines are related.

PRODUCT RECALL

When a manufacturer recalls a product line that it knows or suspects is defective. Cars with faulty steering, frozen drinks contaminated with alcohol and toys with sharp edges are all examples of products that have been recalled

How efficiently and openly a company behaves in such circumstances can greatly affect its brand reputation.

PRODUCTIVITY

The relationship between sales and expenditure, a too-often ignored subject in MARKETING. Marketers have traditionally used resources without looking very closely at the relationship between that use and the resulting sales. Is the cost of increasing the amount of ADVERTISING going to be less than the extra revenue from the resultant increase in sales? If not, then what is the point of it? There may be a point, but the question has to be asked.

PROFIT CENTRE

An organisational unit or function within a company that is charged with producing a profit.

PROFIT IMPACT OF MARKET STRATEGY

Commonly known by its acronym PIMS. An extensive DATABASE that throws some light on the factors that bring about different rates of return on investment (ROI) in different industries. The database arose out of a series of studies undertaken by the US company General Electric in the 1960s.

PROMOTION

A special effort to increase the sales of a PRODUCT.

This may be through a one-off ADVERTISING CAMPAIGN; or through special displays at trade shows and retail outlets; or through competitions broadcast in the MEDIA.

One of the most famous promotions in recent times was dreamt up by British Airways. Described as "The World's Biggest Offer", the airline gave away all its plane seats on one particular day (April 23rd 1991): 25,000 tickets out of London's Heathrow airport and 25,000 tickets in. That was at a cost of £10 million of lost ticket revenue and £6 million of advertising expenditure. Nobody will ever know what extra revenue the promotion brought in.

PROMOTIONAL BUDGET
An estimate of the likely cost of a PROMOTION.

PROSPECT
Any individual to whom a marketer aims to sell a PRODUCT. Marketers do not set out to "prospect for a mine"; they set out to "mine for a prospect".

PSYCHOGRAPHICS
A methodology for segmenting consumer markets that is based on social class (see A,B,C1), LIFESTYLE and personality.

PUBLIC RELATIONS
"The means by which an organisation tries to develop a mutual understanding between itself and its public", according to the Institute of Public Relations. Public relations (PR) is a two-way communication, as much about listening as about telling.

While much PR work is concerned with handling press conferences and press releases, PR covers a wide range of activities, from preparing in-house newsletters to negotiating sponsorship deals. A company's relations with government, with consumer groups, with trade unions and with investors may all appropriately involve PR.

Public relations can either be carried out by in-house public-relations officers (PROS), company employees specifically charged with the task, or subcontracted to a firm of PR specialists. (Many big companies use a combination of both.) Public-relations firms tend to be small. In Europe more than 80% of them employ fewer than 15 people.

PUBLICITY

"The only truly bad publicity is no publicity" goes the old saying, although it is not certain that the UK royal family (for one) would entirely agree with that.

Companies spend a lot of time and money seeking publicity (the attention of the public) for their products. They woo journalists and editors, and take them on foreign trips. And they sponsor sports and arts events that are themselves likely to attract a lot of publicity.

PUSH AND PULL STRATEGIES

Two different ways to move consumer goods through a DISTRIBUTION CHANNEL. Most companies have to use a push strategy to move their products, persuading each member in the distribution channel to stock them.

Large and rich companies, on the other hand, may be able to choose a pull strategy. By investing large sums of money in advertising and sales promotion they can create consumer demand for their product. That demand then acts as a pull to draw the product through the distribution system.

PYRAMID SELLING

A system of selling goods (often household goods like cleaning products or cosmetics) by setting up a pyramid consisting of layers and layers of agents. The first agent sells a stock of the products to a number of other agents (for a commission), and each of them then sells to a number of others (again for a commission), and so (in theory) ad infinitum.

In practice, by the time the pyramid has built up into a reasonable size there are hundreds of agents all over the place, and there is no way that they can sell all the products they hold at a price which will leave them all with a profit. In some countries pyramid selling has been made illegal.

QUALITATIVE RESEARCH

MARKET RESEARCH that is designed to gain insights into a consumer's ATTITUDE, PERCEPTION and motivation. Such research makes no attempt to come up with statistically measured results.

Its methods are chiefly GROUP DISCUSSION and depth interview, and the number of respondents involved in a research session is small, perhaps fewer than 50.

Qualitative research is widely used in new product development in order to elicit consumers' views of what are desirable and undesirable features of the product. It is also frequently used in the early stages of the development of a major research project in order to give the researchers a general feel for the market situation.

Quality is free.
Phil Crosby

QUALITY

A much-discussed subject in management, with almost as many different interpretations of what it means as participants in the discussion. Quality was once something that Japanese products and industrial processes had, and that western ones, by and large, did not have. It was an approach to business and industry that started with the point of view of the customer. From there it aimed to provide products and services that exceeded the expectations that customers had of them. Quality was a measure of the extent to which it succeeded.

It pays to give most products an image of quality;
a first-class ticket.
David Ogilvy

QUANTITATIVE RESEARCH

MARKET RESEARCH that uses SAMPLING techniques in order to arrive at quantitative results. This research reveals what proportion of the population owns video recorders, or how many people watch the latest soap.

AGB, a research firm, suggests that there are only a few basic questions underlying all quantitative market research.

- ❏ Who are you?
- ❏ What do you buy?
- ❏ Where do you buy it?
- ❏ How much?
- ❏ At what price?
- ❏ When?
- ❏ What else could you have bought?
- ❏ Where else could you have bought it?

QUANTITY DISCOUNT

A price reduction given to a customer who buys in large quantities; the larger the quantity purchased, the larger the discount.

Quantity discounts are usually offered by manufacturers to wholesalers. But they can also be offered by wholesalers to retailers. Retail grocery chains negotiate quantity discounts directly with manufacturers because they are able to buy in such large quantities.

QUESTIONNAIRE

The primary tool of MARKET RESEARCH, a device for delivering questions to respondents and recording their answers. It has four main purposes.

1 To collect relevant data.
2 To make data comparable.
3 To minimise bias in the asking of questions and the recording of answers.
4 To frame questions in a varied and interesting way so that respondents will answer without resentment.

The DESIGN of the questionnaire is of great importance to the success of research. It must cover the ground without being too long, and the questions must be easy to understand and not ambiguous. To get the questionnaire right, therefore, it is usual to try out a PILOT before the final version is released for field work.

With a pilot, interviewers conduct the interview in the normal way and note any difficulties that arise. The feedback from the trial is then used to redesign those parts of the questionnaire that cause problems.

I keep six honest serving men
(They taught me all I know)
Their names are What and Why and When
And How and Where and Who.
Rudyard Kipling

QUOTA SAMPLE

A selection of respondents for a piece of MARKET RESEARCH such that age, sex, class, and so on, are represented in the same proportion as in the population as a whole.

RANDOM SAMPLE

A sample from a population which has been chosen in such a way that each member of the population has an equal chance of being chosen. In practice, it is not easy to select such a sample because in all populations some members are less accessible than others; they may effectively make themselves unselectable by being abroad, sick, or just unwilling to participate. Hence, although market researchers would like to use random samples most of the time, in practice they have to rely on some self-selection in their work.

RATE CARD

A list of prices for ADVERTISING charged by a television channel, a radio station, a newspaper or a magazine. A television rate card typically includes the cost of a 30-second spot at different times of day. A newspaper or magazine rate card includes the cost of a full-page or half-page advertisement, plus special rates for the back page, or for the "inside front cover".

Rate cards are used by advertising agencies in planning their use of the MEDIA. They are also of considerable interest to marketing managers with advertising budgets to prepare.

REACH

The proportion of a total MARKET that an advertiser wants to reach at least once in an ADVERTISING CAMPAIGN. If the TARGET MARKET is made up of about 1m people and the reach is 80%, then 800,000 people will have to see the advertising over the given period.

RECALL TEST

A test used by market researchers to find out how much consumers remember about particular advertisements.

Unaided recall tests reveal which advertisements respondents can spontaneously remember. Aided recall tests show which advertisements they can remember from a series that they are shown.

RECOMMENDED PRICE

Many manufacturers recommend to retailers a price that they should charge for their products. This is in part to give price guidelines to retailers operating in the same market, but in the past it has on occasions been more than that.

Manufacturers, fearful that retail price-cutting might create an unstable market, would refuse to supply retailers who charged less than their recommended price. But this practice has now been outlawed in most free-market economies.

RED GOODS

An American expression for FAST-MOVING CONSUMER GOODS. Consumer goods, such as food, that are consumed and replaced at a rapid rate. Compare this with ORANGE GOODS and YELLOW GOODS.

RED LINING

Putting a limit on the geographic or demographic extent of a marketing campaign – for instance, deciding not to distribute a direct mail campaign for Mediterranean cruises among the residents of poor inner-city suburbs.

REFERENCE GROUP

A social group on which consumers model their behaviour. A reference group may be a bunch of friends, neighbours, or colleagues, or it may be a distant group that the consumer admires or aspires to belong to, such as movie stars or pop singers.

The influence of reference groups is strongest where highly conspicuous products are involved, such as clothes, cars, drinks or high-tech equipment. Marketers often attempt to associate such products with their appropriate reference group.

REGISTERED DESIGN

In order to maintain exclusive use of distinctive corporate designs – shapes, patterns, configurations, or unusual ornamentation – companies need to register them.

RELAUNCH

The reintroduction of an existing BRAND on to the MARKET after changes have been made to it (see also REPOSITIONING). For example, in the 1980s Colgate relaunched its Palmolive soap as a PRODUCT for the health-conscious. It underwent some cosmetic changes: a new, softer shade of its original green colour, a more rounded shape and new PACKAGING.

Nabisco relaunched its Shredded Wheat brand without making any changes whatsoever. It simply ran a major ADVERTISING CAMPAIGN that emphasised the dietary qualities of the old product: high fibre, low fat, and no added sugar or salt.

REPERTOIRE

The group of brands within a PRODUCT CLASS which a consumer considers to be acceptable; in other words those brands that he or she will purchase occasionally. Complete BRAND LOYALTY (in which a consumer never buys anything but one particular brand of a product) is very rare.

The British, always more comfortable with dead foreign languages than with living ones, favour Latin for their brand names. For example, the blackcurrant drink Ribena is named after the Latin word for blackcurrant: ribes nigrum.

REPOSITIONING

When a company decides that one of its products is not performing as well as it might because its original (successful) POSITIONING has invited too many competitors, then it may attempt to reposition the PRODUCT. This is will do by changing some of its features, such as its PACKAGING or its price, or even its DISTRIBUTION CHANNEL.

One of the most dramatic repositioning successes in the USA was based on a change of distributor. The Haynes Company renamed and repackaged its line of ladies' hosiery and introduced it as a SUPERMARKET item. As L'Eggs it was a "runaway" success.

R

REPRESENTATIVE SAMPLE
See QUOTA SAMPLE.

RESEARCH BRIEF
A written statement defining the objectives of a piece of MARKET RESEARCH, as agreed between the company that is commissioning the research and the agency that is going to undertake it.

RETAILER
The place where products and consumers finally get together, the last stop on the DISTRIBUTION CHANNEL. Retailers come in many different shapes and sizes, from department stores to corner stores, from hypermarkets to flea markets. There are almost 2m of them in the USA.

A man without a smiling face must not open a shop.
Chinese proverb

ROLLING LAUNCH
The process of gradually introducing a new PRODUCT into the MARKET. The first stage might consist of putting the product through a market test. If it is successful then DISTRIBUTION might be extended, perhaps to another test area. This way the whole market can be be covered gradually.

ROP
See below.

RUN-OF-PAPER
Advertisements that appear in newspapers or magazines in no particular order, that is, they do not have a specified position (such as "facing contents page"). Run-of-paper (ROP) advertisements are less expensive than those that want to be in a particular position. But there is a risk that the advertiser ends up somewhere near the back of the publication facing an article that few people want to read.

SALES FORECAST

An estimate of how much a company hopes to sell to a MARKET, calculated separately for each PRODUCT. A sales forecast forms the basis for establishing a SALES QUOTA.

Forecasting for new products is not easy: it may have to depend on extrapolating from demand for similar products, or on market tests of the product.

Forecasting sales for existing products may be easier, but it still depends on analysing the dynamics of markets that are constantly changing. Statistical tools such as TIME-SERIES ANALYSIS and multiple-regression models (which identify the factors that influence sales) can be employed. But despite these sophisticated techniques, the fingers-in-the-wind judgments of managers and sales people are still widely used.

SALES INCENTIVE

A special reward offered to a SALES PERSON for exceeding a predetermined goal. The reward may be in the form of cash, but it is increasingly common for it to be something like a special holiday, or a trip to an exotic location. A number of travel agents specialise in providing "incentive travel" for large companies and their employees.

Sales resistance is the triumph of mind over patter.
Anon

SALES LETTER

A letter sent to potential customers to remind them of the existence of a particular PRODUCT, or to alert them to the LAUNCH of a new product.

SALES LITERATURE

The collection of published material that is produced by a manufacturer (catalogues, sales letters, advertisements, brochures, and so on) as part of the MARKETING of its products.

SALES MIX

The proportion of different products sold from within a range produced by a manufacturer. Thus a garment manufacturer may have a sales mix of 3y shirts, 2y trousers and y jackets. If the profitability of each is known, the manufacturer can make calculations about how it wants the mix to shift.

SALES PERSON

Someone employed to sell products or services. The terms "sales staff" or "sales representatives" are also widely used. In some industries, like stockbroking, sales people must have a licence in order to carry out their trade.

A salesman has got to dream, boy. It comes with the territory.
Arthur Miller, *Death of a Salesman*

SALES PROMOTION

A special short-term event or offer dreamed up in order to launch (or to relaunch) a product. It may be a reduction in price, a free gift or, for example, for a garden furniture manufacturer, a special stand at the Chelsea Flower Show. The trick is to make sure that the costs of the promotion are more than covered by the margin the extra sales generates. Not all companies get this right. When Hoover offered free flights to UK consumers who bought one of its products the response was overwhelming and cost the company millions and severely dented its image.

The smoothest thing about a used car is the salesman.
Anon

SALES QUOTA

A specification by a company of targets that it expects a SALES PERSON to reach in a given period (usually every quarter). Sales quotas are based on the company's SALES FORECAST; but they may be set higher than the forecast in order to push the sales staff harder. Sales people's earnings are often related to the extent to which they exceed or fall short of their quotas.

SALES RESPONSE FUNCTION

The relationship between likely sales volume during a specified period of time and different levels of MARKETING support. Other things being equal, the higher the level of marketing support (particularly of ADVERTISING and sales PROMOTION), the more of the PRODUCT is likely to be sold.

Marketing managers try to calculate sales response functions (albeit imprecisely) using a mixture of judgment, statistical analysis of past sales and marketing expenditure, and occasional experiments. The experiments are often held in a smallish television region where the results of an increase in advertising expenditure can be easily measured.

SALES TERRITORY

The basic unit of organisation of a sales force. Each SALES PERSON is assigned an exclusive territory in which to sell their company's products. It is their responsibility to develop and cultivate contacts in that territory, and to accept credit (or blame) for the sales performance there.

SALIENT ATTRIBUTE

The aspect of a PRODUCT that is most noticeable to a consumer, and by which the product tends to be judged. Margarine's salient attribute could be said to be its spreadability; a blanket's is its warmth.

SAMPLE

A PRODUCT, sometimes specially packaged, that is given away to consumers, often to persuade them to try something new. Samples can be delivered door-to-door, attached to other products, or given away in retail stores. They are an effective but potentially expensive way of getting a product into the hands of consumers. Procter &

Gamble is believed to have given away 20m samples during the LAUNCH of Vidal Sassoon's Wash & Go shampoo.

The practice of giving away samples has boomed in recent years: 94% of housewives say that they believe in samples; 79% say it is the main reason for purchasing a new product; and 71% say it is the main reason for switching brands (television advertising lags a long way behind at 40%).

SAMPLING

Examining a limited number of a large population so that by studying the part something may be learnt about the whole. The "population" is all those people who have the characteristics in which the researcher is interested.

Sampling has lots of sound statistical theory behind it. Generally speaking, the larger the sample the more accurate the result but the greater the cost of the sampling. Most MARKET-RESEARCH projects do not require very high degrees of accuracy, so samples are usually small. National research on consumer goods will normally not involve more than 1,500–2,000 respondents. Minimal samples would be in the region of 300–500.

The selection of people for a sample can be made in several ways. For purposes requiring the greatest statistical validity a RANDOM SAMPLE is used, involving unbiased means of selection – such as drawing names from a telephone book or from the electoral role. For most market-research projects, however, samples may be chosen more selectively, as in a QUOTA SAMPLE.

SBU

See STRATEGIC BUSINESS UNIT.

SCIENTIFIC MARKETING

A once-fashionable term but a misnomer; not even the most devoted marketers would claim much scientific support for their discipline. Nevertheless, scientific marketing is useful shorthand for the systematic ordering of MARKETING techniques in order to minimise uncertainty in an uncertain marketplace.

SCRAMBLED MERCHANDISING

An expression used mainly in the USA to describe the tendency of retailers to move away from selling specialised goods and towards whatever PRODUCT areas are profitable. For example, drug stores in the USA sell a lot more than drugs; newsagents near offices sell instant coffee; newsagents near schools sell lollipops.

SCREENING

A process of analysing what chances a new PRODUCT has of success by considering the extent to which the product has (or has not) got those elements that will determine its success. For instance, screening a new pizza would involve considering how acceptable things like the thickness of its crust, the variety of its topping, or the flavour of its cheese were to the MARKET at which it was being aimed.

SECONDARY DATA

All information used by market researchers that has not been gathered directly by them: the opposite of primary data. It includes all data collected by governments and commercial research firms, as well as information contained in company records and data gathered previously by other researchers.

The chairman of Revlon once asked his sales force what business they thought they were in. They all replied, "The business of selling cosmetics". "No" he said soberly. "You're in the business of selling dreams."

SEGMENTATION

See MARKET SEGMENTATION.

SELECTIVE DISTRIBUTION

The DISTRIBUTION of products by a manufacturer only to certain specific retailers. For example, only to those who guarantee to buy a certain quantity within a certain time, or to those who agree to give the products prominence in their window display.

SELF-LIQUIDATING OFFER

A type of sales PROMOTION best explained by means of an example: a manufacturer offers customers who buy a PRODUCT (Product A) at its regular price a chance to buy Product B at a price well below its normal price, usually at least a third less.

The customer has to send to the manufacturer some proof of purchase of Product A – a box top, for instance – along with payment for Product B. The manufacturer will have acquired Product B at low cost; as a stock-clearance item or a bulk purchase from another manufacturer, for example. So the price paid by customers who take up the offer, though well below the retail price, will still be high enough to cover the cost of Product B to the manufacturer. The offer, which promotes the sales of Product A, thus pays for itself; it is said to be self-liquidating.

Popular items typically offered by manufacturers in this kind of promotion are T-shirts, mugs or kitchen ware.

The advertising man's only moral obligations are to shift his client's stuff – be it soap powder or politics – and to honour the integrity of the product. The singular and cardinal sin in advertising is the unsubstantiated claim.
Jacques Seguela

SELLER'S MARKET

A situation in which consumers want to buy more of a particular type of goods or services than are being supplied.

Economists say that in such a situation the price of the goods or services will rise, and that this will attract other players into the market. That, in turn, will increase the supply of goods or services to such an extent that it might become the exact opposite: a BUYER'S MARKET.

Such logic does not apply in cases like telecommunications, where the initial capital investment required to become a supplier is prohibitively high. It does not apply either when there are things like import controls that prevent competitive products from entering a market.

SHARE OF VOICE
That proportion of all the ADVERTISING for products in a particular MARKET that is accounted for by a single one of them. Also known by its acronym SOV.

SHELF LIFE
The amount of time that a PRODUCT (particularly foodstuffs) can remain in a saleable condition on the "shelf" of a shop. DATE-STAMPING the product indicates the date on which its shelf life ends and its shelf death begins.

The expression has come to have a wider use: an artless young actress can be said to have a short shelf life as a screen siren; this summer's Gianni Versace evening wear has a shelf life of a season (until it can be resurrected in 20 years' time as a genuine antique).

SHOPPING MALL
A number of individual shops gathered together in one large air-conditioned covered space that has ample parking facilities. Very popular in the United States, shopping malls can now be found all over the world. Their attraction to customers is that they are protected from the weather and from muggers (because they have closed-circuit television and security guards), and they provide easy ways to walk from one shop to another.

SHRINKAGE
A euphemism for the stock in a retail outlet that disappears without being recorded in the cash register. In other words, it is the stock that is damaged, shoplifted, stolen or (in the case of perishables) left over and thrown away or given away.

SIC
See STANDARD INDUSTRIAL CLASSIFICATION.

SIMULATION
The acting out of a real-live MARKETING situation for the purposes of testing a PRODUCT. Two types of simulation are used in marketing.

1 Computer simulation. Data is fed into a computer and the outcome of a range of possible actions compared. For example, an advertiser might want to test the effectiveness of various MEDIA options. A computer simulation could indicate the probable consumer behaviour resulting from various ADVERTISING actions (television commercials at a variety of times, newspaper advertisements on different pages on different days, and so on).

2 Laboratory simulation. This is often used to test BRAND purchasing behaviour, particularly with respect to price. In a simulated store a group of shoppers is invited into a room where they are given a sum of money and asked to spend it on a range of branded products presented to them. After they have completed their purchases they are suitably diverted while the prices on the products are changed. The shoppers are then given another sum of money to spend, and the differences (if any) in their choices are noted.

SINGLE MARKET
The programme of the European Union to make all member states behave as if the whole of the EU were one market. That involves ensuring the free movement within of goods, capital and labour.

For MARKETING experts, the single market programme has presented a number of challenges and opportunities. Most spring from the question: "Can companies now sell their products more widely across Europe?" To answer this manufacturers have to go back and answer a number of other questions first. For example:

● Is their TARGET MARKET in other parts of Europe the same as in their home market?
● Is usage of the PRODUCT or service the same in other countries?

- Does the product have similar distribution channels in all markets?
- Are those markets sufficiently similar to employ the same marketing strategy?

SKIMMING

A PRICING strategy often used when a new PRODUCT is introduced into a MARKET.

New products tend to be price-inelastic, that is, the demand for them is relatively insensitive to price. The price-maker intent on skimming therefore sets a high price for the product in the early stages of its life cycle. That attracts a consumer group which values the prestige of owning something that is newly on the market, or that equates high price with high quality.

As the product matures and sales slow down, the price is lowered in order to attract new customers. Prices may be reduced several times in this process of skimming.

Skimming is particularly appropriate for MARKETING things like cameras, pocket calculators and video recorders.

SLOGAN

A memorable and apposite saying about a PRODUCT that helps keep it at the forefront of consumers' minds. The best slogans are sometimes witty, and often simple. For example:

- Heineken refreshes the parts other beers cannot reach.
- Persil washes whiter.
- Put a tiger in your tank. (Esso petrol)
- It may be December outside, but it's always August under your armpits. (US deodorant)
- Hands that do dishes can be soft as your face. (UK washing-up liquid)
- I dreamed I was Cleopatra in my Maidenform bra.

SMART

A description given to a product that contains some form of embedded "intelligence" in the form of a microchip – for example, the smart card, a plastic card which incorporates a chip onto which is loaded information about personal credit. The card can be used to make purchases, the price of which can be debited against the information on the chip. The card can then, as it were, be "recharged" with credit as and when it gets used up.

Watch out in future for smart fridges (that can tell when you run out of milk, and send a message to the local grocer asking him to deliver some more), and for smart rubbish bins that can read bar codes in order to inform local electronic shops that you have finished your bacon (or whatever).

SOCIAL GRADING

A system for classifying social status. The system in the socially conscious UK was developed for the Institute of Practitioners in Advertising and is based on the occupation of the head of household.

% of pop.	Social grade	Social status	Occupation of head of household
3	A	Upper middle class	Higher managerial, professional
14	B	Middle class	Intermediate, managerial
22	C1	Lower middle class	Clerical
29	C2	Skilled working class	Skilled manual worker
18	D	Working class	Unskilled manual worker
14	E	Lowest level	State pensioner, widow, casual worker

Source: JICNARS National Readership Survey.

In the USA there is no standard system of social grading. Many marketers there consider it a less useful tool for segmenting consumers than systems based on other factors such as LIFESTYLE or neighbourhoods (see ACORN).

SOCIAL MARKETING

MARKETING applied to ideas, causes or practices. Typical examples are anti-smoking campaigns, and campaigns to encourage the wearing of seat belts. Both try to change people's habits.

SOFT SELL

The use of quiet and restrained methods of MARKETING a PRODUCT; for example, advertisements that rely for their effect on associations (of nostalgia, for instance), rather than on the insistent repetition of a BRAND name or SLOGAN. The opposite of HARD SELL.

Inventors, scientists, engineers and academics in the normal pursuit of scientific knowledge, gave the world in recent times the laser, xerography, instant photography, and the transistor. In contrast, worshippers of the marketing concept have bestowed upon mankind such products as new-fangled potato chips, feminine hygiene, deodorant, and the pet rock.

R.H. Hayes and W.J. Abernathy, *Harvard Business Review*, July 1980

SOLUS SITE

Retail outlets that carry the product line of one company only, such as petrol stations. The term "solus user" refers to consumers who use only one BRAND, like the person who drinks only Smirnoff or drives only Jaguars.

SOV

See SHARE OF VOICE.

SPAM

Junk e-mail – electronic messages sent to inappropriate destinations, sometimes with the malicious intent of blocking up corporate messaging systems.

SPECIALIST RESEARCH

MARKET RESEARCH into particular aspects of markets and MARKETING. A.C. NIELSEN specialises in retail

---

audits; other firms specialise in agriculture, children, the MEDIA, motoring, PACKAGING, pharmaceuticals and tourism.

SPONSORSHIP

The subsidising of an event, usually sporting or artistic, by a company for ADVERTISING purposes. Events receiving wide MEDIA coverage bring the sponsoring company's name and its products to the attention of millions of viewers, and at the same time associate it with a pleasurable experience.

Sports sponsorship has grown fast in recent years and now accounts for over 80% of all sponsorship; arts sponsorship has also grown, and is especially favoured by companies not normally associated with culture, for example, banks and oil refiners. Texaco sponsored Saturday afternoon broadcasts of the Metropolitan Opera for many years, and Shell is known for its sponsorship of the arts in the UK.

For some, sponsorship is a way of getting round advertising restrictions. Cigarette manufacturers who are no longer allowed to advertise on television are enthusiastic sponsors of things like motor racing (Marlboro), tennis (Virginia Slims) and cricket (Benson & Hedges).

STANDARD ADVERTISING REGISTER

Two invaluable directories to the ADVERTISING industry in the USA are:

- *Standard Directory of Advertising Agencies*; and
- *Standard Directory of Advertisers*.

They are collectively known as the Red Books, after the colour of their covers.

STANDARD INDUSTRIAL CLASSIFICATION

A standardised classification of industries and INDUSTRIAL GOODS: there is an SIC in the UK and another in the USA. However, although not identical, they are very similar. Both are based on a decimal code, and all government statistics on industrial products in both countries are published under SIC codes.

For example, in the USA a pair of pliers is code number SIC 342311. The first two digits identify the basic industry. The numbers 19–39 are allocated to manufactured goods, with the number 34 belonging to fabricated metal products. The rest of the digits are as follows.

- Third: industry group (2 = cutlery, handtools, hardware).
- Fourth: specific industry (3 = hand and edge tools).
- Fifth: product class (1 = mechanics hand service tools).
- Sixth: product (1 = pliers).

STANDARDISATION
There are two meanings.

1 A process of cutting down the variety of products produced, often to enable a manufacturer to make economies of scale. Some of these economies may be in a company's ADVERTISING budget.

2 The introduction of generally accepted standards for the manufacture and/or sale of products. This may be for genuine reasons of health (as in food PACKAGING) or safety (as in the marking of drug doses). It may sometimes go beyond this and become standardisation for its own sake: a practice that the European Commission is often accused of.

STOCK CONTROL
The management of the inventory in retail and wholesale outlets. Inventory represents unused capital, so skilful stock control involves keeping stock at levels high enough to ensure that goods are available when customers want them, but not so high that capital is tied up unnecessarily. For a RETAILER, stock control is a major factor in determining profitability.

STORYBOARD

A device that shows the bare elements of a television commercial. The board is composed of a series of frames carrying – in sketch or cartoon form – the idea of the commercial and its development.

Storyboards are a fundamental tool in the CREATIVE departments of advertising agencies, and they are also sometimes used in the PRE-TESTING of advertisements.

In 1850 a Bavarian immigrant to the USA by the name of Levi Strauss made a pair of blue jeans with distinctive metal rivets. Levi's were born. They were made of a tough cotton cloth that had first been manufactured in the town of Nîmes in France. The cloth from Nîmes (de Nîmes) came to be called denim.

STRATEGIC BUSINESS UNIT

An autonomous division within a company that is responsible for planning the MARKETING of one of the company's major PRODUCT ranges. Strategic business units (SBUS) are accountable to top management, but are independent of each other. They may well serve completely different markets, grow at different rates, and have different competitors and objectives. Product reduction might be the objective of one SBU, while the addition of a new product might be the goal of another.

STRUCTURED INTERVIEW

An interview in which the interviewer asks questions exactly as they appear in the QUESTIONNAIRE, adding nothing and explaining nothing to the respondent. The respondent may answer only "yes", "no", or "don't know".

This impersonal technique produces data that can be quickly and easily tabulated. But it places a heavy burden on the designer of the questionnaire. Inaccurate data resulting from badly constructed questions may well not be detected.

SUBLIMINAL ADVERTISING

The presentation of an ADVERTISING message in such a way that the consumer is unaware that he or she has received the message; for instance, as an image flashed on a cinema screen for less than 10 seconds, too short a time for it to have registered with the eye.

Subliminal advertising was made illegal in the USA after regulators in the 1950s were frightened by the thought of its potentially manipulative power. However, very little is known about the strength of the trace left in the brain by such messages.

SUCCESSFUL IDEALIST

A type of consumer identified in recent research into lifestyles that are common across Europe. (See LIFESTYLE.)

It is not enough to succeed. Others must fail.
Gore Vidal

SUPERMARKET

A large, high-volume self-service store. Supermarkets are usually operated on a low-margin, high-turnover basis, and now dominate the grocery trade. Supermarkets are beginning to make inroads into other PRODUCT fields as well, including pharmaceuticals and home improvements (DIY).

The supermarket idea was born in the USA. John Hart Ford introduced CASH-AND-CARRY grocery retailing when he started the Great Atlantic and Pacific Tea Company (A&P) food stores in 1912. Then in 1916 Clarence Saunders opened his Piggly-Wiggly stores where he pioneered self-service and customer checkouts.

A supermarket is distinguished from a SUPERSTORE or HYPERMARKET by its smaller size (less than 25,000 square feet) and its greater concentration on food products.

SUPERSTORE

Large modern stores, technically 25,000–49,000

square feet, located next to a free car park large enough to hold at least 250 cars.

Superstores sell foodstuffs predominantly, but up to 30% of their sales area is typically devoted to non-food items, primarily DIY, hardware and motor accessories. There is a fairly fine distinction between hypermarkets, superstores and supermarkets. The difference is mostly to do with size: hypermarkets are the biggest; supermarkets the smallest.

Pile it high, sell it cheap.
Sir Jack Cohen, founder of Tesco

SURVIVOR/SUSTAINER

Two categories in a popular US classification of consumers. (See LIFESTYLE.)

SWOT ANALYSIS

A mnemonic for four key things to be considered in any planning process. A company's:

- Strengths;
- Weaknesses;
- Opportunities; and
- Threats.

Strengths and weaknesses are factors internal to the company – factors such as an excellent service network or an over-extended PRODUCT MIX.

Opportunities and threats are factors external to the company. Careful scanning for new technological developments might reveal opportunities. Threats might be seen to come from changes in consumer behaviour or government legislation.

You can trust a crystal ball about as far as you can throw it.
Faith Popcorn, US futurologist

SYNDICATED RESEARCH

Large-scale MARKET RESEARCH that is undertaken by a market-research firm of its own accord, and is then offered for sale. Syndicated research is not undertaken specifically at the request of a client.

SYSTEMS SELLING

Selling a total system rather than an individual PROD-UCT. A manufacturer of robots will try to sell a robotic system that suits a whole production line, rather than just one robot for a single operation.

Although buying whole systems costs more in the short term, the buyer's hope is that a complete and compatible system will operate more efficiently than a series of components purchased separately.

TACHISTOSCOPE

A device for measuring the extent to which a consumer registers the BRAND (or other relevant information) that is displayed on a packet. The tachistoscope shows pictures of a package for various time periods, and helps researchers to test the effectiveness of its DESIGN, COLOUR or brand name before the PRODUCT is thrown into the competitive world of the SUPERMARKET shelf.

TAMPER-PROOF

Jars and bottles with heat-sealed plastic bands around their necks providing customers with proof that no-one has got into them since they left the factory. Tamper-proofing became popular after a series of incidents where stores were blackmailed by people claiming to have put powdered glass and other lethal things into containers sitting on their shelves.

TARGET AUDIENCE

The audience to whom a particular ADVERTISING CAMPAIGN is directed, defined in demographic terms, by sex, age, income, and so on. Only when a target audience has been defined can the process of MEDIA planning begin.

TARGET MARKET

One or more segments of a MARKET selected for special attention by a company. As consumers become more affluent and more discerning, it becomes more difficult to market products that satisfy the "masses". New products from MARKETING-oriented companies are now usually targeted at specific groups of consumers.

TEASER

A short advertisement that does not reveal the name of the PRODUCT being advertised, but merely advertises that there is more ADVERTISING to come. Such advertisements are designed to "tease" the curiosity of consumers so that they are on the lookout for the full campaign when it arrives.

Teasers are not new. They were used by the

R.J. Reynolds company when it launched Camel cigarettes in 1913. Its teasers had slogans like "The Camels are Coming". When they came they became one of the world's best-selling cigarettes.

TELE-MARKETING

The use of the telephone as a medium for prospecting for sales, for receiving orders and enquiries, and for handling customer complaints. The telephone provides the sort of immediate contact between company and customer that can be effective in maintaining a good relationship over a period of time.

Telephone selling has been common in industrial MARKETING for some time, and is being increasingly used in consumer marketing, especially in the USA.

The advantages of using the telephone for selling are that it reduces wasted sales visits, and it helps to identify good prospects for a follow-up meeting. On the other hand, consumers may on occasion regard it as an invasion of privacy. (See also DIRECT MARKETING.)

TELEPHONE RESEARCH

In most developed countries telephone ownership is universal and 99% of households have at least one phone. That has enabled market researchers to use the telephone to reach large samples of respondents.

Telephone research is more economical than personal interviewing, and most respondents appear to be at least as willing to talk over the phone as they are in a personal interview.

Telephone interviewing was developed as a research method in industrial MARKET RESEARCH. It is often the only way to contact busy executives in their offices. (See also COMPUTER-ASSISTED TELEPHONE INTERVIEWING.)

TELEVISION RATING

A measure of the popularity of a television programme based on various methods of research. In one system, sophisticated equipment is attached to sets in selected homes to record which channel the set is tuned to. A DIARY PANEL is then used to determine how many people are watching the set. Television ratings (TVRS) are calculated by expressing the programme's audience as a percentage of all the households that can receive TV.

TVR can also refer to the percentage of a PRODUCT'S TARGET MARKET that has one opportunity to see its advertisement during a particular campaign. It is a measure of the intensity of the ADVERTISING CAMPAIGN.

TEST MARKETING

An attempt to test a new PRODUCT'S performance in the marketplace by launching it in a limited area. Unlike product testing, test marketing requires that the full intended national MARKETING strategy be simulated within the selected area. In countries with regional commercial television stations, the area chosen for test marketing is often that covered by a single television company.

Full-scale test marketing is expensive and carries no guarantee that a local reaction to the product will be repeated nationally. For these reasons the practice has become less frequent in recent years, but some consumer goods do still first appear under test-marketing conditions.

TESTIMONIAL

The use of a well-known independent person to endorse a PRODUCT. Chefs are often used for food products; Orson Welles became well-known in his later years for endorsing Paul Masson wines; Michael Jordan for Nike shoes.

THRESHOLD EFFECT

Different types of ADVERTISING begin to be effective at different times. With CLASSIFIED ADVERTISING the effect is immediate. With most other forms it takes time (and money) before an advertisement is noticed against the background "noise" of other advertisements. All money spent on advertising is wasted until this "threshold" is reached. Any company not prepared to spend enough to pass the threshold should not spend anything.

TIME-SERIES ANALYSIS

A technique used in sales forecasting. Historical sales data are analysed in an attempt to discover the reasons for fluctuations in sales over time. Any causal relationships thus uncovered can then be used to help forecast future sales.

TNC

See TRANSNATIONAL CORPORATION.

TOLL-FREE NUMBERS

Telephone numbers that people can call for free; the charges are paid by the person being called. Toll-free numbers have proved a valuable marketing tool in encouraging consumers to find out about or purchase products and services over the telephone.

TRADE DISCOUNT

The means by which members of a DISTRIBUTION CHANNEL (the "trade") are paid for their services. Manufacturers offer wholesalers discounts on their list prices, and the wholesalers in turn discount their prices to retailers. Such discounts, because they are given for functions performed, are also called functional discounts.

Trade discounts may also be related to the speed at which goods are expected to sell.

In addition to a trade discount, manufacturers sometimes offer wholesalers a QUANTITY DISCOUNT. It is also normal to offer a discount for prompt payment, known as a cash discount. A cash discount might be expressed as "3/14 net 28", which means the buyer (WHOLESALER or RETAILER) will be given a 3% discount if payment is made within 14 days, and that in any case the bill must be settled within 28 days.

TRADE FAIR

See EXHIBITION.

TRADE-IN ALLOWANCE

A price reduction given for a used product when a similar one is purchased new; an indirect form of price cutting. In car retailing, for example, prices advertised by dealers may appear to be uniform. But fierce price competition takes place between them when the trade-in allowance is being negotiated. In the case of durable household goods (cookers, refrigerators, and so on) trade-in allowances are often nominal.

TRADEMARK

A name, design or logo peculiar to a business or its products. It doesn't have to be registered for a business to claim it as theirs but it does have to be distinctive.

TRADING STAMPS

Free stamps given by retailers in proportion to the value of purchases made. The stamps are usually redeemable for catalogue merchandise or cash. Retailers sometimes have their own stamps, or they purchase them from trading-stamp companies. Trading stamps are fast being replaced by an electronic form of bonus given for loyalty to a particular retailer or wholesaler. (See LOYALTY CARD.)

TRADING UP

MARKETING slang for moving UPMARKET.

TRAFFIC

The department in an ADVERTISING AGENCY that controls the flow of work between one department and another; ensuring, for example, that the production of a television commercial is synchronised with the production of print advertisements, and that both can appear simultaneously in the MEDIA as part of a co-ordinated campaign.

TRIAL OFFER

A form of PROMOTION that gives away a small SAMPLE of a PRODUCT in order to persuade consumers to make their first purchase of the product. Often used with cosmetics and foodstuffs.

U&A

See USAGE AND ATTITUDE.

Uhu is German for the particular sort of eagle owl that frequents the valley where the glue of the same name is made.

UNDIFFERENTIATED MARKETING

The MARKETING of a PRODUCT to the widest possible MARKET, appealing to needs that unite consumers rather than divide them. For many years Coca-Cola very successfully marketed only one product in one kind of container. Henry Ford revolutionised automobile production when he mass-produced the Model T for an undifferentiated market: one model for everybody, in any colour as long as it was black.

Nowadays undifferentiated marketing has largely given way to the concept and practice of MARKET SEGMENTATION. Even Coca-Cola produces a range of Cokes, plus Fanta and Sprite. It also produces them in large bottles, small bottles, plastic bottles and glass bottles. Likewise there are now cars to suit every taste, although they retain a link with Henry Ford's ideas of mass production by developing differentiated exteriors on a core of undifferentiated engines.

When the Burroughs computer company bought Sperry it ran a competition among its employees to find a new name for the combined outfit. The winner chose Unisys, and a headline in the Wall Street Journal *asked, "If this was the winning name, what could possibly have lost?"*

UNIQUE SELLING PROPOSITION

The idea – less popular than it used to be – that a PRODUCT should have at least one unique feature that differentiates it from all its competitors, and that can be easily communicated to consumers through ADVERTISING. But uniqueness is rare, and coming up with a continuous stream of products with unique features is, in practice, very difficult. So the unique selling proposition (USP) has given ground to newer ideas like POSITIONING that are less tied to actual product features.

UNIT PRICING

A form of PRICING used by retailers to enable shoppers to make price comparisons between products. In the USA, in particular, large retailers (especially supermarkets) show the price per unit of a PRODUCT in addition to its total price.

For example, a grocer might carry four brands of instant coffee, each BRAND available in three different sizes. Unit pricing enables the consumer to see that a 4oz jar of Brand A costs 50 cents an ounce, while an 8oz jar of the same brand costs 47 cents an ounce. But an 8oz jar of Brand B may cost 46 cents an ounce, while a 4oz jar of Brand B costs 52 cents an ounce.

UPMARKET

Sometimes called Upscale in the USA. A popular term that (like its counterpart downmarket) refers to the structure of a MARKET, visualised as having a top and a bottom, and a way to move up and down. This dimension can apply across different criteria.

	Upmarket	**Downmarket**
Class	Upper	Lower
Price	Expensive	Cheap
Style	Exclusive	Mass
Quality	High	Low
Features	Luxury	Basic

Marketers use the term chiefly with respect to product POSITIONING and REPOSITIONING. Going upmarket might involve increasing the quality of the product – manufacturing in Italy, say, rather than Hong Kong – and limiting its DISTRIBUTION to exclusive speciality shops.

USAGE AND ATTITUDE

A comprehensive study of a MARKET, including

quantitative measures of actual consumer behaviour, and qualitative measures of consumers' attitudes to different products in the market. Also known by its acronym U&A.

USP
See UNIQUE SELLING PROPOSITION.

VALS
See below.

Velcro was invented by a Swiss gentleman who wondered how sticky burrs became attached to his clothes. Its name is short for VELours-CROché, French for "hooked velvet".

VALUE ADDED
An expression that has become popular since the advent of value-added tax. "Where's the value added," people ask of new business plans or processes as they are proposed. It refers to little more than what has been added to a product or service to justify an increase in its price.

VALUE ANALYSIS
A technique designed to help a company find ways to reduce its costs without sacrificing its PRODUCT's market appeal. For example, MARKETING managers and production and DESIGN engineers get together to discuss ways that costs might be cut. Their ideas are ranked according to their cost-saving potential, and are analysed for feasibility. Any proposed change is then checked against consumer perceptions of the product's value.

Value analysis can be applied to new product ideas when they are still at the design stage, as well as to existing products.

VALUES AND LIFESTYLES
A US classification of consumer behaviour developed by the Stanford Research Institute and commonly abbreviated to VALS. (See LIFESTYLE.)

The word "Valium" is quite meaningless, as are the names of other famous Roche drugs like Librium and Mogadon.

VARIABLE PRICING
The selling of the same PRODUCT or service at different prices depending on the time or location.

Variable pricing is not very practical for large manufacturers of INDUSTRIAL GOODS, but it is a practice that is often found among street markets or antique sellers. For example, the prices of fruit on a market stall may be higher on Saturday mornings than they are on Thursday afternoons; the price of an antique may be higher for the well-dressed American tourist than it is for a local dealer.

When buyers don't fall for prices, prices must fall for buyers.

Anon

VIRTUAL MALL

A series of shopping sites (web sites, that is) that have been gathered together electronically on the INTERNET. A person looking at the "pages" of one of these shops will be electronically led into the pages of another, and so on, throughout the virtual mall.

VOICEOVER

The addition of a voice to a filmed advertisement. Voices are important to the overall impression given by an ad; beers and such macho things love to use Orson Welles sound-alikes. But the most famous voices on advertisements do not get to see the exotic locations that are invariably shown behind their voices. They rarely travel further than the recording studios of large city centres.

Appropriately, Vespa is Italian for wasp.

WARRANTY
See GUARANTEE.

WEB SITE
A location on the World Wide Web (www), the global collection of interconnected text and graphics that can be accessed via the INTERNET.

WHEEL OF RETAILING
An American theory of retailing based on the fact that retailing is constantly changing. The theory states that most new retailers start as low-status, low-margin, low-price operators. As they prosper they move UPMARKET, leaving opportunities for new entrants.

The theory has some explanatory value. Many discount stores that started after the second world war progressed upmarket thereafter. The Gap began by selling cheap jeans to teenagers; now it has over 300 stores in the USA and Europe that are style-setters for the young and middle-aged alike. Others are now filling the gap left by The Gap and selling jeans cheap.

WHITE GOODS
Washing machines, refrigerators, freezers and cookers: durable goods that at one time were always encased in white enamel.

WHOLESALER
An intermediary linking manufacturers and retailers. Full-service wholesalers used to dominate business in both the USA and Europe, providing warehousing, a sales force, a delivery service, credit, MARKET RESEARCH and help with reordering. But competitive pressures reduced the importance of these all-in-one intermediaries.

In some cases manufacturers themselves have taken over the wholesaling function, using their own DISTRIBUTION centres to supply retail outlets. In other cases, new-style wholesalers have successfully limited the services they offer to retailers (as in CASH-AND-CARRY wholesaling). In yet other cases, full-service wholesalers have moved into retailing, setting up chains of independent retailers that only they supply.

WORD-OF-MOUTH ADVERTISING

It is every marketer's dream to have a PRODUCT so satisfactory to those who purchase it that they immediately tell their friends and neighbours about it. Just as immediately, those friends and neighbours then go out and buy it, and they too tell their friends and neighbours. Such word-of-mouth advertising is very powerful and can make or break a Hollywood movie.

YELLOW GOODS

An expression used in the USA for consumer goods that are bought infrequently, last for a number of years before needing to be replaced, and are generally expensive. They include the sort of things that come under the category of both WHITE GOODS and BROWN GOODS: ovens, fridges, televisions or music sets. Yellow is thus a mix of brown and white.

Historically, the letters "X" and "O" have been unusually popular in trade names. But few are as rich in them as Oxo and Xerox. The word Xerox comes from xeros, the Greek for dry, being the first copying process not to use wet ink.

YUPPY

A sociological classification that came into common parlance in the 1980s, and that had special significance for the marketers of fast cars, clarets and faraway holidays.

Yuppy is short for "Young Upwardly Mobile Professional Person", a well-educated breed with a high income and a high propensity to seek instant gratification, even if it means borrowing heavily to do so.

The 1980s sprouted several other such acronyms; for example, Dinkies (households with Double Incomes and No Kids); Droppies (Disillusioned, Relatively Ordinary Professionals Preferring Independent Employment Situations); and the Puppy (the Previously Upwardly Mobile Professional Person).

The American locksmith Linus Yale, who invented the combination lock in 1862, had nothing to do with Elihu Yale who founded the university of the same name.

ZAP

The practice of using a remote-control device to switch back and forth between one television channel and another. Zapping is a nightmare for advertisers and market researchers. First, it enables viewers more easily to switch away from advertisements when they are showing; second, it throws into chaos any attempt to measure rigorously which programmes an audience is watching, and for how long (see DIARY PANEL). Seasoned zappers with butterfly minds can (in all honesty) say they are watching two programmes at once.

Your legacy should be that you made it better than it was when you got it.
Lee Iacocca

Part 3
APPENDIXES

1 Biggest advertising agency groups, 1996

	Worldwide gross income ($billion)
WPP Group	3.42
Omnicom	3.04
Interpublic	2.75
Dentsu	1.93
Young & Rubicam	1.36
Cordiant	1.17
Grey	0.99
Havas Advertising	0.97
Hakuhodo	0.90
True North Communications	0.89

Source: Advertising Age.

2 Top 10 advertisers in the United States, 1995

	$billion
Procter & Gamble	2.77
Philip Morris	2.58
General Motors	2.05
Time Warner	1.31
Walt Disney	1.30
Sears Roebuck	1.23
Chrysler	1.22
PepsiCo	1.20
Johnson & Johnson	1.17
Ford Motor Co.	1.15

3 Number of computers per 100 population

USA	31.9
Australia	22.1
Canada	22.1
Norway	22.0
Finland	20.3
Denmark	19.5
Sweden	18.2
UK	18.2
Netherlands	17.0
New Zealand	17.0

Source: The Economist Pocket World in Figures.

4 Worldwide advertising expenditure

	%
Above-the-line	40.0
Print	20.3
Television	14.4
Radio	3.1
Cinema	0.1
Outdoor	2.1
Below-the-line	60.0

5 Advertising expenditure as a % of GDP

Costa Rica	1.57
Hong Kong	1.44
New Zealand	1.44
Panama	1.42
South Korea	1.33
Jamaica	1.31
Greece	1.26
Australia	1.25
Taiwan	1.23
USA	1.23

6 Expenditure on television advertising, 1995

	$billion
USA	31.5
Japan	16.2
Germany	4.9
UK	4.2
France	3.3
Italy	3.0
Brazil	2.7
Argentina	2.0
Spain	1.8
South Korea	1.7

Source: Worldwide Advertising Trends.

7 Top 10 US magazines by advertising revenue, 1996

	$billion
People	526
Sports Illustrated	522
Parade	494
Time	439
TV Guide	403
Newsweek	384
Better Homes & Gardens	335
PC Magazine	318
Business Week	298
PC Week	239

Source: Advertising Age.

8 Consumer spending by category, 1995 (%)

	Food, drink, tobacco	Clothing, footwear	Housing	Fuels	Household goods & services	Health	Transport communications	Leisure & education	Others	Total
Australia	21.6	5.2	17.5	2.1	6.4	8.0	14.7	10.6	13.9	100
Brazil	35.1	5.2	23.7	5.2	4.4	4.6	7.3	4.0	10.5	100
France	18.2	5.6	18.0	3.7	7.5	10.3	16.8	7.5	12.4	100
Germany	16.4	6.5	18.7	3.8	8.8	6.3	16.1	10.9	12.4	100
Hong Kong	14.0	22.4	13.5	1.1	12.6	3.9	12.2	8.6	11.7	100
Italy	20.2	9.5	13.9	4.3	9.1	7.1	12.7	8.7	14.7	100
Japan	17.5	5.3	22.3	…	5.0	11.3	11.0	10.8	16.9	100
Poland	41.9	5.3	2.8	5.3	1.7	3.5	8.3	7.8	23.3	100
Portugal	34.4	9.7	8.0	…	5.6	2.7	13.0	5.5	21.2	100
Sweden	19.7	5.7	29.2	5.4	4.9	3.9	15.5	9.3	6.2	100
UK	19.5	5.8	16.1	3.3	6.4	1.7	17.8	10.1	19.3	100
USA	17.0	5.2	14.1	2.7	4.7	15.8	11.1	12.0	17.3	100

Source Euromonitor

9 The top global brands

1 Coca-Cola
2 Kellogg's
3 McDonald's
4 Kodak
5 Marlboro
6 IBM
7 American Express
8 Sony
9 Mercedes-Benz
10 Nescafé

Source: Interbrand.

10 The best US business schools for marketing

1 Northwestern
2 Vanderbilt
3 Michigan
4 Harvard
5 Indiana
6 UCLA
7 Columbia
8 Wharton
9 Dartmouth
10 Stanford

Source: Business Week, October 1996.

11 Recommended reading

Arnold, D., *The Handbook of Brand Management*, Pitman, 1992.

Baker, M.J. (ed.), *The Marketing Book*, Heinemann, 1987.

Broadbent, S. and Jacobs, B., *Spending Advertising Money* (4th edition), Business Books, 1984.

Bureau, J.R., *Brand Management*, Macmillan, 1981.

Chisnall, P.M., *Strategic Industrial Marketing*, Prentice-Hall, 1985.

Chisnall, P.M., *Marketing Research* (4th edition), McGraw-Hill, 1992.

Chisnall, P.M., *Consumer and Buyer Behaviour* (2nd edition), McGraw-Hill, 1992.

Cutlipp, S.M., Center, A.H. and Broom, G.M., *Effective Public Relations* (6th edition), Prentice-Hall, 1985.

Davidson, H., *Offensive Marketing* (revised), Penguin, 1990.

Donnelly, J., and George, W.R., *Marketing of Services*, American Marketing Association, 1981.

Engel, J.F., *et al.*, *Consumer Behaviour* (5th edition), Dryden, 1986.

Greenley, G.E., *The Strategic and Operational Planning of Marketing* (7th edition), McGraw-Hill, 1987.

Hofstede, G., *Cultures and Organisations: Software of the Mind*, McGraw-Hill, 1991.

Humphrey, G., *The Professional Adviser's Guide to Marketing*, Mercury, 1990.

Kotler, P., *Marketing Management: Analysis, Planning and Control* (7th edition), Prentice-Hall, 1991.

Kotler, P. and Armstrong, G., *The Principles of Marketing* (6th edition), Prentice-Hall, 1991.

Kotler, P. *et al*, *The New Competition*, Prentice-Hall, 1985.

Lancaster, G. and Massingham, *Essentials of Marketing*, McGraw-Hill, 1988.

Levitt, T., *The Marketing Imagination*, The Free Press, 1983.

Levitt, T., "The Globalisation of Markets",
   Harvard Business Review, May–June 1983.

McDonald, M., *Marketing Plans*, Heinemann,
   1986.

McDonald, M. and Leppard, *Marketing Audit*,
   Heinemann, 1991.

McDonald, M. and Leppard, *How to Sell a Service*,
   Heinemann, 1988.

McRae, C., *World Class Brands*, Addison-Wesley,
   1990.

Miller, R.B. and Heiman, S.C., *Strategic Selling*,
   Kogan Page, 1989.

Murphy, J., *Brand Strategy*, Director Books, 1990.

O'Shaughnessy, J., *Competitive Marketing*, Allen
   & Unwin, 1984.

Porter, M., *Competitive Strategy*, The Free Press,
   1980.

Sheth, J., "Marketing Megatrends", *Journal of
   Consumer Marketing*, Summer 1983.

Van Mesdag, M., *Think Marketing*, Mercury,
   1988.

Van Mesdag, M., "Winging it in Foreign Markets",
   Harvard Business Review, Jan–Feb 1987.